The Prediction of
Corporate Earnings

Research for Business Decisions, No. 38

Gunter Dufey, Series Editor
Professor of International Business and Finance
The University of Michigan

Other Titles in This Series

The Prediction of Corporate Earnings

by
Michael F. van Breda

umi
RESEARCH PRESS

Produced and distributed by
UMI Research Press
an imprint of
University Microfilms International
Ann Arbor, Michigan 48106

A revision of the author's thesis,
Stanford University, 1979

Library of Congress Cataloging in Publication Data

Van Breda, Michael F.
  The prediction of corporate earnings.

  (Research for business decisions ; no. 38)
  A revision of the author's thesis, Stanford University,
1979.
  Bibliography: p. 119-124.
  1. Corporate profits.   I. Title. II. Series.

  HG4028.P7V36 1981   658.1'554   80-28975
  ISBN 0-8357-1157-9

Contents

List of Tables

List of Figures

Preface

Much research proceeds within a well-defined and broadly accepted framework. Its concern may be to extend the boundaries of already documented theories. Alternatively, it may involve new empirical evidence to support previously proposed hypotheses. In some cases, research may consist, essentially, of dotting i's and crossing t's.

The same is true of books. In general, a book appears only when the state-of-the-art has settled out and the ideas it contains have become relatively well-established. This is an inevitable concomitant of the tremendous speed with which new ideas are being generated. As a result many texts tend to be surveys of a field and, in effect, to draw the closing lines around the field.

This book is different in that it constitutes a beginning rather than an ending. Surprisingly little is known about the behavior of corporate earnings. The research reflected here is an initial attempt to open up a new avenue of inquiry in this area. By its very nature, then, it is not a completed line of endeavor. The research suggests a thrust, a new approach. In no sense, though, can it claim to provide a final solution; that must await much work by many other researchers.

The book will have achieved its modest aim if it succeeds in stimulating research in the area of corporate earnings predictions. Profits are central to a free-enterprise economy. On the one hand, they sustain and reward past investment, and on the other, they are the prime motivator of present investment. Since current investment is a function of earnings expectations, our ability to forecast earnings is of critical importance to the efficient functioning of our economy. Much research is needed to achieve the goal of effective forecasting. This text suggests fruitful lines of research to reach that goal.

The essential direction is that to predict corporate earnings we need to build a causal model that explains the dynamics of earnings behavior. This model draws on the economic theory of competition, on the one hand, and on accounting theory, on the other. It suggests that to understand accounting earnings we need to model the accounting system as a filter and explore how economic events are mediated by this filter.

Numerous people assisted greatly in this effort. Naming individuals is always invidious. Nevertheless, three groups played a central role and deserve special mention. The idea evolved at Stanford University under the guidance of Professor William H. Beaver, who was my thesis supervisor. The work would not have been possible without his insights, advice, and encouragement. Professors Dick Wittink and John Shoven were extremely supportive. I am indebted to many others at Stanford. Among these are Dean Robert Jaedicke, Professors Joel Demski, Charles Horngren, William Sharpe, and James Patell. A special debt is owed to Professor Thomas Hofstedt, now at SMU, for his patience and understanding, and to my friend and colleague Robert Maki.

My colleagues at the Alfred P. Sloan School of Management at MIT have played a vital role in seeing this work to its conclusion. I am particularly indebted to Dr. Morris McInnes and Professor Peter Brownell for their support. My secretary, Christine Hardiman, bore the brunt of numerous drafts efficiently and cheerfully.

My thanks too to Ernst and Whinney whose generous financial assistance made my research possible.

Finally, I am indebted to my family in a way that no words can express. None of this would have been possible without the support and tolerance of my wife, Nancy, my son, Adrian, and my parents, Donald and Rene.

The final result, needless to say, reflects only my own inadequacies. Ultimate responsibility for its flaws is mine alone.

Cambridge
November 1980

1

Introduction

American business generated an estimated $121.5 billion in after-tax profits during 1978. No other single aggregate is a better index of the nation's economic health. As Adam Smith recognized over 200 years ago, the "propensity to truck, barter, and exchange" in pursuit of profit is the glue that binds together the intricate network of social relationships in a free-enterprise society.

Profits, or at least the expectation of future profits, are the primary cause of all investment. Individuals save money because they expect to have it returned with interest. They invest their money in businesses in the hope of future dividends. Businesses invest these funds in research and development, property, plant, and equipment in search of profits from which, in turn, dividends and interest will be paid.

Without profits, there can be no dividends, no interest, no incentive to save, and ultimately no new investment. Without new investment, the nation's competitiveness in world markets must decline, standards of living must fall, and employment opportunities for the nation's citizens must shrink. Much depends, therefore, on today's corporate profits and our expectations of tomorrow's. They are the engine of all economic activity.

The trend of profits is of direct concern to many constituents of society. The managements of businesses are directly responsible for borrowing funds, investing them at a profit, and ensuring the payment of dividends. In a free-enterprise society, they are delegated to search out and select profitable opportunities. Their measure of success is the degree to which they can generate profits. Management, thus, has a direct interest in estimating the trend of profits in their corporations.

The investment community as a whole, consisting, as it does, of private individuals, pensioners, pension-fund trustees, bankers, and so on is intimately concerned with future profitability. Whoever has monies invested must be concerned with future dividends, and, therefore, with the trend of profits.

Estimates by the investment community of future profitability can shape the economy quite profoundly. As various industries appear to promise greater future returns so capital will flow into the firms in those industries. Those areas that promise less can be expected to shrink as capital dries up. The net result is a shift of resources from one segment of the economy to another.

Government, too, is intimately concerned with corporate profitability. For one, corporate profits are a source of much government revenue. Corporate income tax in 1973, for instance, totalled $35 billion, or 16% of total tax collections. They are thus an important source of revenue making it essential for government planners to be able to predict future profits.

Government has a further interest. In this, as in many countries, it has a responsibility to maintain employment at a level that is as near to full as possible. As profits fall in a sector so investment will fall, and with it employment possibilities. Labor must move out and transfer into those sectors where expectations of profits are greater. Government can assist in this if it can identify areas of future profitability.

Labor, and by implication the public-at-large, cannot be indifferent to profit trends. As financial resources shift in search of greater profits, so labor must move in search of employment. In this past decade, for instance, much capital has shifted from the older cities in the Northeast to the so-called Sun Belt. The result (and, in part, the cause) has been a massive migration of people to the Southwestern regions of this country.

Certain industries (e.g., steel in recent years, and, going further back, textiles and footwear) have revealed discouraging trends in profitability. These industries have declined as a result, creating high unemployment and forcing labor to move into other growth industries where future profitability appears more assured. To the extent that labor is aware of these trends, it can locate itself in industries where employment opportunities are greatest.

In short, while the contents of a book such as this may appear superficially arcane and of specialized interest only, the results are of direct and intimate concern to almost everyone in our society. We are all affected by the profitability of corporations. Our standard of living, our way of life, our wages and salaries, our pensions, our tax burden, and the forms of employment we undertake, are all shaped by corporate profitability. Since all these facts involve choices with long-term effects, our ability to peer into the future and predict corporate profitability is of great importance to us all.

Today's profits are a reward for yesterday's investment. They are also one indicator of future profits. One way, therefore, to estimate future profitability is to extrapolate past profits. All other things being equal, firms which have been profitable will continue to be profitable. The reality, however, is that things are seldom equal. Technology, population, government intervention, even changing weather patterns all ensure that tomorrow is seldom like today.

If, therefore, we do want to predict future profitability, it becomes essential to understand the impact on profits of these factors. A knowledge of the causal forces that affect profits will substantially enhance our ability to predict and, hence, to plan. To the extent that one can identify changes in causal factors, and their effects on profitability, one's predictions must improve.

A model of the behavior of profits would represent a sorely needed supplement to the planning activities of businesses and the investment community. Yet in spite of the apparent importance of a causal understanding of future profits to management, the investment community, government, and the public at large, it is extraordinary how little progress has been made in building such a model. This text suggests how we might begin to create such a model.

Underlying it is the belief that causal model-building is feasible. This is not a foregone conclusion, but a basic hypothesis that only future work can confirm or deny. It is conceivable, for instance, that firms are subject to a multiplicity of small forces none of which is of particular importance. This would suggest that the best predictive model could be at best a statistical model. On the other hand, the impact of the forces might be so specific to each particular firm that nothing can be said in general terms.

The underlying hypothesis of this work is that there are a few causal forces at work that affect all firms and in such a way that general statements can be made. In particular, the effect of competition on all firms in the economy is traced. The essential claim is that competitive forces cause all abnormal profits to be driven out of the economy. In the long run, therefore, all firms become equally profitable effectively.

This effect is mitigated by the fact that our index of profitability is accounting earnings. The second leg of the model tries to capture the effect accounting measures have on profitability. Since this is of interest to accountants, the importance of the prediction of corporate earnings to accounting practice and theory is documented below and a brief survey of the relevant accounting literature is then offered.

Why Prediction?

Some recent authoritative statements of current official thinking in accounting are contained in the Trueblood Report (1973) and the FASB's Tentative Conclusions on Objectives of Financial Statements (1976). Both assume that the value of a common share equals the discounted stream of future dividends, including capital gains, expected by investors.

What they suggest is that

$$p = \int_{t}^{\infty} q_s^e \exp[- \int_{t}^{\infty} \varrho_u^e du] ds$$

where p = value of the share
q_s^e = expected quasi-rent or dividend
and ϱ_u^e = expected discount rate

They suggest that investors will want to predict this stream of benefits and the earnings stream on which it is based and will rely upon published financial reports, among other sources, for that purpose. In the words of the Trueblood Committee:

> An objective of financial statements is to provide information useful to investors and creditors for predicting, comparing, and evaluating potential cash flows to them in terms of amount, timing, and related uncertainty.

And since the earning power of an enterprise is the source of future cash flows to the investor, the Committee goes on to suggest:

> An objective of financial statements is to provide users with information for predicting, comparing, and evaluating enterprise earning power.

Or in the words of the FASB's Tentative Conclusions:

> Financial statements of a business should provide information about the economic re- sources of an enterprise, which are sources of prospective cash inflows to the enterprise; its obligations to transfer economic resources to others, which are causes of prospective outflows from the enterprise; and its earnings which are the financial results of its opera- tions and other events and conditions that affect the enterprise.

This study is clearly in the spirit of the Trueblood Report and the FASB's Tentative Conclusions in its attempt to gain insight into the stochastic behavior of earnings in order to arrive at a model that will permit superior predictions of prospective earnings when compared with models extant in the literature using a mean square error criterion.

A more general justification for this study may be derived from state preference theory. Given certain assumptions, investors may be assumed to have utility functions, which they maximize by the allocation of current wealth to present consumption and state-contingent claims to future consumption. The role of information in this context is to enable investors to revise their assessments of the probabilities of the occurrence of future states. The value of such information derives from its use in the more primary allocation of wealth.

A special case of this general state preference model assumes either quadratic utility functions or normal probability distributions, and state-inde- pendent prices to arrive at a mean-variance model. In this framework the value of a security is a joint function of its end-of-period expected return and its asso- ciated risk commonly referred to as beta. The role of information in this con- text is to permit the prediction of beta.

Beaver, Kettler, and Scholes (1970) demonstrated that the security price beta is correlated with a similarly defined accounting beta. Crudely, fluctua- tions in security prices are related to fluctuations in accounting income. Thus, there is reason to believe that a better understanding of the behavior of accounting earnings might lead to better predictions of security risk.

Conversely, if one assumes a value of beta, a theoretical price for a stock, conditional on the expected market rate, can be adduced. Ball and Brown (1968) have shown empirically that the provision of the underlying net income figure before its publication, were it possible, and if it diverged from its expectation, would enable the investor to earn an abnormal return in the market. The divergence of net income from its expected value may therefore be considered information.

By the rational expectations hypothesis, all users of accounting information can be expected to extract the underlying generating function from the earnings stream and use this to arrive at an expected income figure. Unfortunately, due to paucity of data and the possibility that generating processes vary across firms and maybe over time, identifying the processes has proved difficult for empiricists. One hopes that a deeper understanding of the theory of the behavior of earnings will obviate some of these empirical problems and enable one to build models that will permit a better-justified prediction of earnings than accounting researchers have been able to provide to date.

A Literature Survey

The interest of accountants in the area of the stochastic properties of earnings began with the work of Beaver (1970) and of Ball and Watts (1972). In the course of a series of statistical tests, they compared two broad classes of models. The first came to be known as the mean-reverting model and was written:

$$X_t = \mu + u_t \tag{1.1}$$

where X_t is the annual earnings, μ is a constant, and u_t is a random variable with expected value zero. That is, earnings in any year are assumed to fluctuate about a mean, which can be thought of as the permanent underlying earnings stream. This model is consistent with the premises of most studies of income smoothing where it is hypothesized that management tries to eliminate year-to-year fluctuations.

The second class of earnings behavior models came to be known as the martingale. It suggests that our best estimate of next year's earnings will be this year's earnings. For an example, consider the random walk

$$X_t = X_{t-1} + u_t \tag{1.2}$$

The important difference is that this process does not have a constant mean. Each year we have a new mean, which is in fact last year's realization. Given this model, there is no obvious reason to expect any kind of constant underlying deterministic earnings stream. The two models have very different implications for accounting:

1) Smoothing is both possible and perhaps desirable if the earnings stream is mean-reverting. Attempts at smoothing may fail, however, if the earnings stream is a martingale process, as a result of the lack of an underlying constant stream.

2) If the process is mean-reverting, there may be an underlying long-term trend to earnings, which the accountant might seek to reveal by segregating extraordinary items that could be considered random fluctuations. On the other hand, if the process is a martingale, there can be no such justification for the separation of extraordinaries, and, failing other arguments, an all-inclusive approach to net income would appear more appropriate.

3) If the process is a martingale, the expectation of all future income streams is the present income realization. On the other hand, if the process is mean-reverting, income can be expected to revert to an already known and established long-term trend. Thus, in the sense that a change in a martingale indicates something permanent, while a change in a mean-reverting process indicates something transitory, changes in the former may be said to contain more information. This is an important distinction when interpreting changes in income.

The mean-reverting model was rapidly discarded for series such as sales, net income, and earnings per share. The distinction was also drawn between martingales that were random walks, and others that were autoregressive processes. The essential technique used was to estimate autocorrelations and to attempt to identify a model such as the random walk from these statistics. The predictive power of the model so identified was then tested by Ball and Watts (1972) *inter alios*. Most results pointed to a random-walk model or an autoregressive model with parameter close to one. These have since come to be known as naive models since they imply that this year's earnings are our best estimate of next year's.

These rather *ad hoc* procedures gave way to the Box-Jenkins techniques. A series of papers using these techniques has emerged in the last few years— *inter alios* Watts (1975), Dopuch and Watts (1972), Griffin (1975), Foster (1977), Albrecht, Lookabill, and McKeown (1975). Clearly these techniques expanded the number of models under consideration. Lorek, McDonald, and Patz (1976), for instance, claim to find evidence of models as diverse as a first-order simple moving average to a mixed process involving lags up to seven years.

The models so derived are devoid of economic theory and are in fact only sophisticated smoothing techniques. As such, they add very little to our understanding of the process generating earnings. If our primary goal is simply to generate forecasts based on past observed earnings numbers, they might be considered satisfactory. However, even as pure forecasting techniques, they are limited. Lorek et al., for instance, report quite dramatic shifts in the models selected when only one or two periods of data are added to the series. The models appear to be very sensitive to the addition of fresh data to the front of the series, e.g., to adding 1977 data to a series that had ended in 1976. This is possibly due to the fact that accounting earnings appear to follow something close to a random walk, so that from a predictive point of view, the most recent earnings are the most important. Since these models are so sensitive to changes in data, they are unsuitable for extrapolation purposes.

Attempts to offer explanations for the results observed have all centered on the exogenous disturbance term. It has been suggested that the martingale model reflects a sequence of events with permanent impacts on the firm, while the mean-reversion reflects a sequence with no future inpact at all. These are clearly polar extremes. Moreover, it is difficult to believe that one firm experiences only temporary fluctuations, while another experiences only permanent disturbances. Add to that the implicit suggestion that one but only one of these occurs each year, and the explanations become inadequate.

Beaver (1970) is the only author to attempt to add some theory to this model-building process. His model stands midway between the two above extremes, permitting events to have a semipermanent effect on the firm, a far more appealing notion. In his words:

> . . . there is good reason to believe that accounting measurement rules permit, and in many cases, *dictate* that unexpected components in earnings be averaged over several subsequent periods. For example, consider a situation where there has been an unexpected change in the probability distributions of the future net cash flows associated with depreciable assets, such that the value of those assets has changed substantially. In the model described earlier, that change in asset value would be reflected in the unexpected component of the rate of return (and undeflated earnings). However, because historical costs, not net present value, are used as a basis for recording depreciable assets and their expiration, only a portion of that change will be implicitly reported in the current period and the rest will be spread over the remaining useful life of those assets.

The model that he proposed to capture this phenomenon assumed an underlying economic generating process that was reverting, i.e.,

$$A_t = \mu + u_t \tag{1.3}$$

He then suggested that the random disturbances u_t were smoothed by the accounting system to yield an observed model of the form

$$A_t = \mu + 1/n \sum_{i=0}^{n-1} u_{t-i}$$

(1.4)

The model suffers from the same deficiency as all the others in this genre—the u_t are wholly undefined, exogenous disturbances. Nonetheless, the suggestion is a valuable one and reappears in the model proposed in this study.

2

A Theory of the Firm

The previous chapter provided the justification for our interest in the stochastic behavior of corporate earnings. This chapter outlines a theory of the firm that provides insight into how earnings might be expected to behave. The underlying assumptions are presented first and the Marshallian theory is then outlined. Several of the points raised in this section are then dealt with more explicitly in the remaining sections.

Assumptions and Definitions

Consider a private economy at a point in time, denoted the present, consisting of a fixed, finite number of consumers, a fixed, finite number of producers, and a fixed, finite number of commodities. The fixing of commodities and consumers is immaterial to the theory, but the fixing of the number of firms creates a monopoly that, in conjunction with decreasing returns, creates the possibility of pure profits or rent, which is the topic of this chapter and the main theme in this study.

Assume further that at each period in the future, uncertainty may be captured by a set of mutually exclusive possible states to which the actors in the economy, more particularly the consumers, attach probabilities. The commodities are then characterized in terms of their physical properties, the date and location at which they will be available, and the state in which they obtain. Importantly, they are assumed to be infinitely divisible. Where this does not hold, discontinuities can occur, giving market power to individual participants and leading to the breakdown of perfect competition.

To each commodity so defined may be attached a parameter p_j, which denotes the present price an actor has to pay for delivery of one unit of commodity j at the date, location, and in the state detailed in the contract. Markets are assumed to be complete except when stated otherwise.

Consumers are assumed to be Savage rational and to be noncolluding. They are assumed to be costlessly informed at all times of the prices of all commodities. Producers are also assumed to be noncolluding and to be costlessly informed of the prices of all commodities. Producers manage firms characterized by activity vectors

$$y^k = (y_{1k}, y_{2k}, \ldots, y_{nk}) \tag{2.1}$$

where y_{ik} = units produced or used of the i_{th} commodity by the k_{th} firm. There are no externalities of production, i.e., each input-output vector depends only on the firm's own technical possibilities. The set of feasible vectors for each firm forms a production set Y_k, which is characterized by the following assumptions:

1) $0 \in Y_k$ $\hspace{6cm}$ (2.2)

2) $Y_k \cap (-Y_k) \subset \{0\}$ $\hspace{5cm}$ (2.3)

3) $Y_k \supset (-\Omega)$ $\hspace{5.6cm}$ (2.4)

4) Y_k is convex $\hspace{5.5cm}$ (2.5)

The last assumption includes both decreasing and constant returns to scale. Decreasing returns lead to the existence of positive pure profits or rent. This is a corollary of an earlier assumption that the number of firms is fixed, which implies an effective monopoly for firms. To escape this dilemma, it is customary to assume that constant returns to scale operate in the long run when profits throughout the economy are driven to zero.

Managers are assumed throughout to be profit maximizers, i.e., they are assumed to choose that vector y^{k*} such that for all $y^k \in Y_k$

$$p \cdot y^{k*} \geq p \cdot y^k \hspace{5cm} (2.6)$$

It should be noted here that the term profit is used variously by different authors. Some make it synonymous with the normal return to capital. Others use it to denote the sum of the return to capital and any excess return that capital earns above and beyond its normal return, where normal may be defined in this context as the marginal value product. Still others denote as profit only the excess of abnormal return that capital earns. This profit, sometimes termed pure profit, is often ascribed to a monopoly held by the capitalist, since it is a fundamental thesis of perfect competition that profit in this sense will tend to zero. Except where the context is clear, I shall distinguish between pure profits (in the sense of rent or abnormal earnings) and profit (the sum of pure profits and normal profit or the return to capital).

The boundary of the production set is the production function, which may be denoted

$$h_k(y_{1k}, y_{2k}, \ldots, y_{nk}) = 0 \hspace{4cm} (2.7)$$

For simplicity, it is often assumed that each firm produces only one output. It is assumed that there are a large number of firms in each industry so that each firm supplies only a small amount of the total output and demands only a small fraction of the total inputs.

Given the set of prices, it is possible to associate with each production function $f(\cdot)$ a cost function $C(\cdot)$ that traces the locus of least cost output for all levels of the output y_{1k}. For example,

$$C = C(y_{1k}) \text{ for all } y_{1k} \in Y_k \tag{2.8}$$

In the long run all costs are assumed to be variable. In the short run, however, one or more of the inputs may be nonvariable, i.e., they do not appear in the production decision of management, which leads in turn to fixed costs. Fixed costs are closely related to the assumption of a fixed number of firms, which may be fixed by virtue of an assumed immobility of capital in the short run. This leads, from the law of diminishing returns to scale, to the existence of rent. This rent accrues to the fixed factor.

Together, these constitute one set of sufficient conditions for perfect competition to hold. They are not, of course, necessary conditions which, although formally unknown, may be summarized informally as those conditions that lead the economy to behave "as if" the above conditions held. Many have criticized the above assumptions as unrealistic. In the light of logical positivism, such criticisms are irrelevant since a positive theory stands or falls by its predictions rather than by its assumptions.

The Zero-Profit Condition

By way of introduction, and in the light of what follows with relatively little loss of generality, assume a firm producing a single output, under certainty and perfect competition, with fixed costs and with decreasing returns to scale in the relevant range. By the assumption of profit maximization, each manager seeks to maximize net revenue, i.e.,

$$\max_{q} pq - C(q) - f \tag{2.9}$$

where q is units of output, $C(\cdot)$ is variable costs, and f fixed costs. This leads by differentiation to the well-known first order condition that the firm should produce q^* such that

$$p = C'(q^*) \tag{2.10}$$

i.e., price equals marginal or variable costs. Fixed costs are clearly irrelevant in establishing the optimal production level.

Marshall (1920) argued that in the short run the size and number of firms are fixed. In effect, the individual firm's overhead, usually made up of capital items, is fixed. Since price is a parameter, it is possible that the resulting contribution $(p - C')\, q^*$ is insufficient to cover the overhead in which case the firm goes out of business. The result is to lower the pressure on factors lowering variable costs and to decrease output supply, thereby raising prices. The combination of these two effects will raise the contribution of the firms now on the margin in the industry to a point where it equals the overhead.

Alternatively, the contribution might cover overhead with some to spare, leading to the existence of pure profit. This last is true because the economist, unlike the accountant, includes the normal return to capital as a cost of production. Any revenue that is in excess of costs, therefore, must be pure profit. Where it exists, entrepreneurs may be expected to enter the industry in search of it. As they do, output prices can be expected to fall with the increase in supply, and costs of production to rise with the increased demand for factors of production. Ultimately, supply will reach a point where the contribution is equal to the overhead for the marginal firm. As before, a zero-profit condition will obtain for firms on the margin.

In familiar diagrammatic terms Figure 2.1 shows the cost curves of a marginal firm on the left and the industry supply and demand curves on the right.

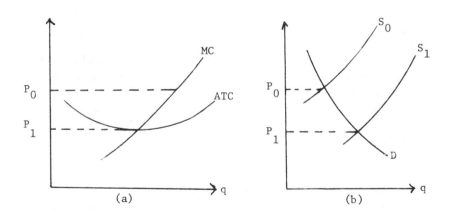

Figure 2.1.   (a) Productive Equilibrium for the Firm;
(b) Market Supply and Demand Curves.

First-order optimality conditions for the firm clearly hold at either price, and at a price of p_0, supply will balance demand if supply is s_0. The only condition not satisfied at this price is that of zero profits. Entrepreneurs will enter the industry and force the price (in this diagram) down to p_1, where price equals average cost and the last condition obtains. Simultaneously the supply will shift to the right and a new market equilibrium will obtain.

There are thus three equilibrium conditions in the long run. First, all firms must set marginal cost to price. Second, the market supply and demand must balance. Third, firms on the margin must earn zero profits. This last is made possible by the assumption of mobile resources, or stated differently, the assumption of free entry.

To these three conditions must be added a fourth, since we have not yet assumed zero profits across the entire industry. Inframarginal firms—those firms who are more efficient—will still be making positive profits. For those to disappear, we must assume that investors will buy up existing firms, rather than create new ones. The outright purchase of the inframarginal firm raises the cost curve (of the purchaser) to a point where it is a tangent to the price line, ensuring that with the economic rent included zero pure profits are earned.

It should be mentioned here that the existence of inframarginal firms may be ascribed in general to the existence of inelasticities of supply. If one assumes, therefore, that in the long run these inelasticities will disappear, then in the long run, causes of rent will disappear, ensuring in the long run that all production functions exhibit constant returns to scale or, equivalently, ensuring that, in the long run, all firms are, in effect, marginal and earn zero profits. This assumption that inelasticities of supply will disappear in the long run will be used below.

In all that follows it is vital to distinguish between zero profits on the margin and zero profits across the industry. The former is induced by what one might term *real investment*. The latter is induced by takeovers, or what one might term *financial investment*. The distinction is the subject of the next chapter.

An alternative formulation of the above argument makes explicit use of the production function rather than the cost function. As before we assume certainty and, for simplicity and without loss of generality, a single good economy and two dates—the present and the future. We assume that the firm draws on its owners for this period's consumption goods c_0, which it uses as inputs to its productive process. It returns to them consumption goods in the next period c_1, which they may, by assumption, trade freely in an exchange market. Prices for this period's and next period's commodities are p_0 and p_1, respectively, and such that the effective market rate of interest is

$$r = (p_0/p_1) - 1 \tag{2.11}$$

Note that these are present value prices.

The output q_1 in period one may be assumed to be a function of the input $-q_0$, say $f(q_0)$. Then the firm is assumed to maximize the difference.

$$p_1 f(q_0) + p_0 q_0 \tag{2.12}$$

where q_0 is measured along the negative axis, which is achieved when

$$f'(q_0) = -p_0/p_1 \tag{2.13}$$

But since the budget line may be written as

$$W_0 = c_0 + (p_1/p_0)c_1 \tag{2.14}$$

or as

$$c_1 = (-p_0/p_1)c_0 + W_1 \tag{2.15}$$

the above condition simply states that at the optimum, the production function is a tangent to the budget line. (See, by way of example, Figure 2.2 (a).) Its equivalence to the short-run Marshallian condition is obvious from the two diagrams below.

Figure 2.2.   *(a) Intertemporal Productive Equilibrium for the Firm;*
                     (b) Traditional Short-Run Equilibrium.

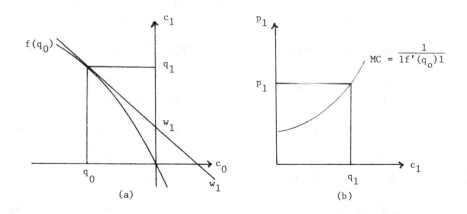

The slope of the production curve is the marginal rate at which c_0 can be converted into c_1. Its absolute inverse, therefore, is the marginal cost of producing c_1. Using c_0 as the numeraire it follows that the above condition simply states that

$$MC = 1/|f'(q_0)| = p_1 \qquad (2.16)$$

It is identical to the Marshallian condition derived earlier.

By analogy with the earlier formulation, it should be noted that this is only the marginal condition appropriate to the firm itself. The quantity W_0 is a measure of the profit being earned by the firm, i.e., the pure profit or excess return. This follows since

$$W_0 = q_1/(1+r) + q_0$$

$$= p_1 f(q_0) + q_0 \qquad (2.17)$$

the precise quantity the firm set out to maximize. But this is clearly positive, i.e., pure profits exist. Entrepreneurs, as before, will therefore enter the industry in search of these profits, causing the price p_1 to fall as supply increases. Ultimately, the price will rise to a point where the marginal firm earns no profit.

Again it should be noted that I have not assumed zero profits across the entire industry. Inframarginal firms will still be making positive profits. For those to disappear we must assume that investors will buy up existing firms. The price at which they will be prepared to do this will be W_0 of course, since this is the present value of these firms. Diagrammatically, the following situation will then hold where W_0 has now become a fixed cost of the firm. Clearly by equation (2.17) above profit will now be zero.

Figure 2.3.   Productive Equilibrium for the Firm (Long Run)

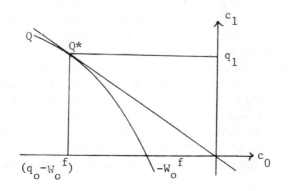

The above argument can clearly be extended to the general case of multiple time periods, uncertainty, and multiple commodities. We assume as before that markets are complete and that managers

$$\max_{y^k} p \cdot y^k \tag{2.18}$$

But given that the vector p consists of prices to be paid now for future delivery, the vector product is no more than the net present value of the firm or production plan. If this is positive, pure profits are being earned and entrepreneurs will enter the industry until the marginal firm shows a net present value of zero. Investors will purchase the inframarginal firms so that they, too, will show a net present value of zero when the capitalized rents are imputed to costs. Effectively constant returns to scale will rule at this point, and the zero-profit condition will have been obtained. In other words, in long-run equilibrium, we must have

$$p \cdot y^k = 0 \quad \text{for all } k \tag{2.19}$$

This is a fundamental result of perfect competition.

It is convenient at this stage to assume that the commodities in production in period one, i.e., at the outset, are inputs, and the commodities in all other periods are outputs. Correcting the signs we can then write as an equilibrium condition

$$-\Sigma_j p_{1j} y_{1j} + \Sigma_{t=2} \Sigma_s \Sigma_j p_{tsj} y_{tsj} = 0$$

$$\text{or} \quad \Sigma_j p_{1j} y_{1j} = \Sigma_t \Sigma_s \Sigma_j p_{tsj} y_{tsj} \tag{2.20}$$

But the right-hand side is no more than what is normally called the present value of a production plan (expected present value here since it includes uncertainty), and the left-hand side is the "cost" of the project, which we shall denote P_0. In other words, in capital budgeting parlance, in equilibrium, the cost of the project will equal its expected present value. This result will be used in the section that follows.

It has been assumed throughout that managers will maximize the net present value of the production plan. This can be shown to lead to a Pareto optimal economy *inter alia* under certainty and when markets are complete. Implicit, too, is the assumption that capital markets are perfect and that there are no constraints on borrowing or lending. Once one allows for incomplete markets or capital constraints, the value maximization rule is no longer Pareto optimal. The separation between production and consumption decisions can no longer be maintained, and direct use must be made of utility functions. Since the theory of incomplete markets and market imperfections is so ill-specified at present, besides being extremely situational, this book assumes that markets are sufficiently complete to warrant the approach used.

The term "sufficiently" complete needs defining. Arrow (1971) has shown that it is not necessary to have a market in every time-state-type commodity. All that is necessary is a set of state-contingent securities, which enable one to allocate sufficient wealth to each state to purchase the commodities whose prices in those states are known, i.e., if

$$\bar{p}_{tsj} = \text{price of commodity } j \text{ in state } s \text{ at time } t$$

$$\hat{p}_{ts} = \text{price now of the } s_{th} \text{ security at time } t$$

chosen so that

$$p_{tsj} = \hat{p}_{ts} \bar{p}_{tsj} \tag{2.21}$$

then equation (2.20) reduces to

$$P_0 = \Sigma_t \Sigma_s \Sigma_j \hat{p}_{ts} \bar{p}_{tsj} \, y_{tsj}$$

$$= \Sigma_t \Sigma_s \hat{p}_{ts} q_{ts} \tag{2.22}$$

where q_{ts} = wealth required in state s at time t to purchase the required commodity. This term is what may be called a state-contingent quasi-rent, and the $\hat{p}_{ts}$ is the discount factor appropriate to the probabilities of the state's occurrence. This reduces the number of markets required dramatically.

Arrow (*ibid.*) has further shown that where risks are individualistic, i.e., where each individual faces his own peculiar set of states, prices are proportional to the probabilities of the state's occurrence, i.e., equation (2.22) becomes

$$P_0 = \Sigma_t \Sigma_s p_t^1 \pi_{st} q_{st}$$

$$= \Sigma_t p_t^1 \Sigma_s \pi_{st} q_{st} \tag{2.23}$$

where π_{st} = the probability of state s at time t

$$= \Sigma_t p_t^1 q_t^e \tag{2.24}$$

where q_t^e = the expected quasi-rent at time t, i.e., one can reduce the number of prices needed even more dramatically, since all that one needs are the present value prices of a riskless security. Arrow himself describes the result as rather startling, but argues cogently that the economy is probably closer to individualistic risk than it is to systematic risk.

In conclusion, it might also be stressed that the economic theory developed here is intended only as an underpinning to Bain's theory of barriers to entry. In the sense that he relied entirely upon a Marshallian framework, the theory developed here already goes well beyond Bain's own approach.

Rate Equalization

As a corollary to the zero-profit condition, there exists the rate equalization theorem. Stigler (1964) has claimed that this theorem is the most important in economics. In his words:

> There is no more important proposition in economic theory than that, under competition, the rate of return on investment tends toward equality in all industries.

To derive this theorem we first assume certainty and make use of equation (2.20) above as an equilibrium condition, i.e., in long-run equilibrium

$$P_0 = \Sigma_t \Sigma_j p_{tj} y_{tj} \tag{2.25}$$

Consider now a production plan involving a single good so that

$$P_0 = \Sigma_t p_{tj} y_{tj} \tag{2.26}$$

and define

$\bar{p}_{tj}$ = the price of commodity j at time t

ϱ_{tj} = the discount rate between time t and the present appropriate to commodity j

$= \bar{p}_{tj}/p_{tj} - 1$

Thus we can write (2.25) as

$$P_0 = \Sigma_t \bar{p}_{tj} y_{tj} (1 + \varrho_{tj})^{-1}$$

$$= \Sigma_t q_t (1 + \varrho_{tj})^{-1} \tag{2.27}$$

where q_t = the quasi-rent obtained in period t. If for convenience we run t from 1 through T making 0 the present, then it is easy to show that

$$P_0 = q_{1j}(1+\varrho_{1j})^{-1} + \Sigma_{t=2}q_{tj}(1+\varrho_{tj})^{-1}$$

$$= q_{1j}(1+\varrho_{1j})^{-1} + (1+\varrho_{1j})P_1 \tag{2.28}$$

whence

$$\varrho_{ij} = q_{1j}/P_0 + P_1/P_0 - 1$$

$$= q_{1j}/P_0 + (P_1-P_0)/P_0 \tag{2.29}$$

To see the force of (2.29) assume the existence of a money rate of interest i_1 in the first period. The owner of \$1 cash can earn the amount of i_1 in interest in a single period. Alternatively, he can purchase $1/P_0$ of the production plan, earn quasi-rents of q_{1j}/P_0 in the period, and then dispose of the asset at a price P_1/P_0. In equilibrium these two courses of action must of course be equal, i.e.,

$$1+i_1 = q_{1j}/P_0 + P_1/P_0 \tag{2.30}$$

$$i_1 = q_{1j}/P_0 + (P_1-P_0)/P_0 \tag{2.31}$$

However, a comparison of (2.29) and (2.31) reveals that in equilibrium

$$i_1 = \varrho_{1j} \tag{2.32}$$

Since this holds for one commodity j, it must hold for all commodities, i.e., in equilibrium

$$i_1 = \varrho_{ij} \quad \text{for all } j \tag{2.33}$$

This expression states that in equilibrium, the discount rate on all assets or production plans will equal the money rate of interest. Equivalently, there will be a tendency for all rates to equalize over time. Or in other words, if we allow inelasticities of supply to disappear, then in the long run there will be a tendency for all rates to equalize. This is a result that is absolutely fundamental to all that follows and as we have seen it depends crucially on the zero-profit condition for its fulfillment.

Note incidentally that the above result enables us to simplify (2.25) considerably. We have

$$P_0 = \Sigma_t \Sigma_j p_{tj} \, y_{tj}$$

$$= \Sigma_t \Sigma_j \, q_{tj} \, (1 + \varrho_{tj})^{-1}$$

$$= \Sigma_t \, (1 + \varrho_t)^{-1} \Sigma_j \, q_{tj}$$

$$= \Sigma q_t (1 + \varrho_t)^{-1} \tag{2.34}$$

A similar type of simplification holds, as we have already seen, in the case of uncertainty. In each state, the state-contingent commodities may be reduced to a single state-contingent security, making it necessary to know only the discount rate appropriate to that security. Clearly by the above argument it must be true that the discount rate for the security and for all the commodities in that state must equalize. In the terminology of Miller and Modigliani (1958), the discount rates in each risk class must equalize. Moreover, these rates must adjust one to another so that the return and risk are balanced across the various risk classes.

To illustrate this last, consider the CAPM, which is a special case of the state preference model. If one assumes that the world consists of a now and then, that prices are independent of states, that all individuals have identical probability beliefs and quadratic utility functions, then it follows that

$$\varrho_j^e = i + \beta_j (\varrho_m^e - i) \tag{2.35}$$

where

ϱ_j^e = the expected discount rate appropriate to security j

ϱ_m^e = the expected discounted rate appropriate to the market

i = the riskless rate of interest

β_j = cov $(\varrho_j^e, \varrho_m^e)$

= systematic risk of the security

That is, all *ex ante* rates must adjust until they conform to (2.35). To see the force of this define

P_j = the price of security j

$X_j^e = q_{1j}^e + p_{1j}^e$

= the expected total payout at the end of the period

σ_{xj}^2 = the variance of the security payout

Then by definition it follows that

$\varrho_j = X_j/P_j - 1$

$\varrho_j^e = \Sigma \pi_j \varrho_j$

$\quad = \Sigma \pi_j (X_j/P_j - 1)$

$\quad = X_j^e/P_j - 1$ (2.36)

where π_j = the probability of various values of ϱ_j.

Similarly one can show that

$\sigma_j = \sigma_{xj}/P_j$ (2.37)

where σ_j^2 = the variance of the return

whence it follows that

$\varrho_j^e = \{X_j^e/\sigma_{xj}\}\sigma_j - 1$ (2.38)

For example, prices of securities must adjust until they are linked by equation (2.38). Graphically one has the situation shown in Figure 2.4, that is the return on the security will move up and down the line with ordinate -1, by a series of price changes, until it reaches a point where the locus of the security and the market is a tangent to the security price line with its ordinate of i. At this point, the return on the security will have "equalized," with due allowance being made for risk.

Figure 2.4.   Security Market Equilibrium

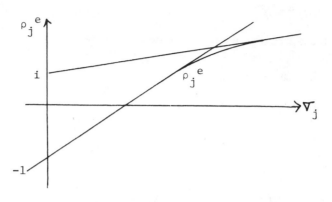

To summarize, in the long run the activity of entrepreneurs and investors will ensure that no abnormal profits are being made in the economy. When this point is reached the cost of a plan and its present value will be equal. Given this, it is possible to show that under certainty, all discount rates will equalize and that the same will hold in each state under uncertainty. Moreover, under certainty these state-contingent discount rates will adjust so that risk and return are balanced throughout the economy. One form of this last is given by equation (2.35), which will be used in the empirical work that follows.

Investment Lags

The argument has been made by Bain (1956) and others that in certain industries entry is *not* free; *structural* barriers to entry exist, which enable the industry to maintain prices above a long-run equilibrium value and lead to excessive profits in the industry. It is also widely held that firms in industries with high barriers to entry indulge in limit pricing, whereby they set prices above the long-run equilibrium values but sufficiently below the short-run equilibrium value to forestall the entry of competitors.

Bain's discussion of barriers to entry proceeds essentially in terms of four factors. These are economies of scale, product differentiation, absolute cost advantages, and capital requirements. To these he adds industry concentration as a parallel factor. Mann (1966) uses these same factors in his later reexamination of Bain's findings and his own classification of additional industries.

For economies of scale to impose a barrier to entry, one presupposes a U-shaped average total cost curve with an optimal plant size that demands a substantial share of the market and fairly steep diseconomies at lower levels. As they point out, it is important to distinguish regional industries from national industries. Cement, for instance, is a distinctly regional industry with an optimal plant taking perhaps 1% of the national market, but 4 or 5% of the regional market it serves. Clearly it is the latter figure that is the relevant one in determining the barrier to entry. The assumed barrier here is the difficulty of gaining a large market share.

On the surface, economies of scale are closely allied to absolute capital requirements. Market share, however, is not closely correlated with absolute capital requirements. Steel plants, for example, require vast capital outlays, while occupying a relatively small share of the market. This factor presupposes, of course, that it is more difficult to raise $500 million than $50 million, which is probably a matter of opinion. Discussed by Bain, but abandoned because of lack of evidence, is the related possibility that borrowing costs vary at different levels. This would have suggested further imperfections in the capital market.

The widespread prevalence of brand names and the vast sums of money spent to develop, promote, and protect them form the basis for Bain's stress on product differentiation as a potential barrier to entry. Not only must capital be found to erect a plant, but sufficient capital must be available for the promotion of the product and its brand name. Further, the differentiation of products also leads to potential market segmentation, implying that the effective market share for optimal entry is substantially larger than a national or industry percentage might suggest. There is probably a scale effect here, too, with firms moving in at a low level requiring relatively little promotion compared with those moving in at a large optimal level. The lack of perfect substitutability between two brands of the same product creates a partial monopoly situation, which might or might not be exploited by existing firms.

Bain, incidentally, suggests that promotion costs might explain the existence of multiplant firms. Economies of scale and absolute capital requirements clearly refer to establishments or plants only. Many, if not most, firms consist of a number of establishments, with often two plants erected on the same site. Economies of scale do not explain this phenomenon. It is, however, conceivable that economies of sales promotion might explain it.

To these three factors and their interaction, Bain adds absolute cost advantages. These derive largely from factors such as control over inputs or special techniques. For example, there is a shortage of limestone deposits, placing existing backward-integrated cement manufacturers in a fortunate position vis-a-vis newcomers. Iron ore sources are controlled by a handful of firms. Automobile manufacturers are often so integrated into parts and subassemblies that it is virtually impossible for an outsider to enter the industry.

Patents are the classic example of absolute cost advantages because they make it possible to control superior techniques.

The table below shows the ranking on these four factors of the industries used in this study as judged by Bain and Mann. Both the individual and the overall rankings are judgmental. A roman numeral I indicates a high barrier to entry while a III indicates a low barrier, i.e., relatively free entry.

Table 2.1.   Barriers to Entry

Industry	Scale-Economy Barrier	Product Differentiation Barrier	Absolute Cost Barrier	Capital Requirement Barrier
Cigarettes	III	I	III	I
Drugs	III	I	n.a.	II
Automobiles	I	I	III	I
Cement	II	III	III	II
Steel	II	III	I	I
Copper	n.a.	III	I	n.a.
Coal	III	III	II	II
Textile mills	III	III	III	III
Containers				
Metal	n.a.	II	III	III
Glass	III	III	III	III

As Mann points out, concentration (monopoly or oligopoly) is the usual reason given for above-average returns. The monopolist is able to manipulate supply to arrive at a price that is above the competitive price. Oligopolists are able to achieve the same, but to a lesser degree. Empirical examination reveals that this factor is not a complete explanation of observed rates. According to Bain and Mann, one has to take barriers to entry into consideration as well. The monopolist faced by potential entrants to his industry might well expand supply and lower his price to discourage this competition. Conversely, one expects highly concentrated industries with large barriers to entry to show high rates of return. The automobile industry and the cigarette industry reveal just that. On the other hand, industries like steel, copper, cement, and containers, while having an eight-firm concentration ratio above 70%, have relatively low barriers to entry and show a correspondingly low rate of profit.

Great care needs to be taken in using concentration ratios. With the number of mergers that have occurred in the past decade, most organizations have diversified to the extent that industry differences have become blurred. In recent years, for instance, as much as 70% of Anaconda's profits have come from its coal subsidiary Peabody, suggesting, perhaps, that Anaconda should be reclassified as a coal company. In fairness to Bain and Mann, they attempted to select only those companies that had specialization ratios above 50%. Those interested in the effects of diversification are directed to the study by Rhoades (1973).

I have argued in the preceding section that in the long run and when resources are freely mobile, i.e., when there arc no barricrs to entry, that the rate of return earned on all assets will tend to equality with one another and with the market rate of interest in turn. Or allowing for risk, I can say that the return earned on a productive asset will tend, in the absence of barriers to entry, to the appropriate risk-adjusted rate of interest in the long run.

Where barriers to entry exist, this equality will hold approximately only. To model this last assume that positive profits are currently being earned in the industry. The total return on the asset, therefore, will exceed the appropriate market rate. If no entry occurs at all, or equivalently, no investment, the return will *ceteris paribus* remain at its current level. If entry is free, the return earned will fall to the market rate, i.e., the appropriate long-run equilibrium rate. If entry is semi-free, i.e., a certain amount of investment occurs, the rate will fall to a point between the current and the market rate. As Stigler says:

> If it is correctly anticipated that without additional investment the rate of return next year will be 10 per cent, the longrun equilibrium rate being 7 per cent, then such an amount of investment may (and, if possible, will) be undertaken that the *expost* rate will be only 7 per cent.

Clearly if the current return being earned is below the expected long-run rate, disinvestment will occur, and the return will move up by an amount depending on the ability to disinvest. All of this is captured by the partial adjustment model:

$$r_t \;=\; r_{ot}^{\,e} + \lambda(\varrho_t^{\,e} - r_{ot}^{\,e}) \quad \lambda \in [0, 1] \tag{2.39}$$

where

r_t = observed rate

$r_{ot}^{\,e}$ = *ex ante* no investment (= no adjustment) rate

$\varrho_t^{\,e}$ = *ex ante* equilibrium (= full adjustment) rate

with $r_t = \varrho_t^{\,e}$ whcn $\lambda = 1$

and $r_t = r_{ot}^{\,e}$ when $\lambda = 0$

Implicit in (2.39) is the assumption that expectations are realized. To escape this assumption, it seems sufficient for our purposes to simply include a residual error term, u_t, i.e.,

$$r_t = r_{ot}^e + \lambda(\varrho_t^e - r_{ot}^e) + u_t \tag{2.40}$$

For the moment, though, we will ignore this error term.

One way to see the force of (2.39) is to revert to the Fisherian diagram, which is given in Figure 2.5. We assume that the firm is at a long-run equilibrium position with investment q_0 and earning zero profits. The production function is a tangent to the budget line at that point, as it should be, and its present value is correctly zero. If we now assume that the market rate changes—say due to a revision in the risk premium appropriate to the firm—the firm needs to undertake investment of Δq to bring it to the new equilibrium point q_0'. At that point, the marginal rate on investment will equal the new market rate. If, however, barriers to entry exist and the investment program is incomplete, the firm will be at a point between q_0 and q_0', where the slope of the production function is greater than that of the new budget line, i.e., the marginal return being earned will exceed that of the market rate as predicted by the model (2.39). The argument is clearly reversible.

Figure 2.5.   Changes in Productive Equilibrium

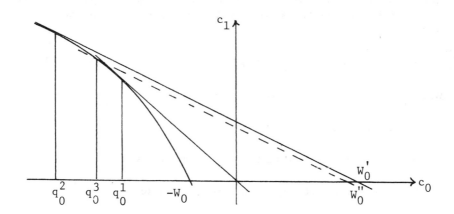

The argument may be extended from the marginal rate to the average rate by my earlier hypothesis that, in the long run, inelasticities of supply will disappear. In other words, in the long run there is a tendency for average rates of return to tend to equality. Equation (2.39) may therefore be interpreted in terms of average rates, as well as marginal rates, although the former process may reasonably be expected to be slower than the latter.

The transition from marginal rates to average rates is essential if one wishes to interpret the empirical results offered in favor of the hypothesis of barriers to entry. The literature on this subject uses average rates of return and purports to demonstrate that high average rates of return are associated with high barriers to entry. Clearly it would be more satisfying if one had access to marginal rates of return. However, these are not available to the empiricist who must therefore work with average rates and the long run.

Combining the literature on barriers to entry, where no models are offered to justify their high rate—high barrier arguments, and the zero-profit rate equalization argument of Marshall and Fisher, which led to equation (2.39)—one may offer as a null hypothesis that high barriers to entry will be associated with low values of λ. Alternatively stated, barriers to entry and the adjustment parameter on this hypothesis will be negatively correlated. This hypothesis is tested in this study.

Conclusion

To sum up then, I have established the following formal economic propositions, which are clearly equivalent and which will be used in the next chapter to provide an explanation of how accounting rates may reasonably be expected to behave.

Making due allowance for risk, provided that resources are freely mobile and elastic in supply, then in an industry where established firms are being operated at a profit, entrepreneurs will enter until

1) All profits disappear.

2) All returns on assets are equal to one another and to the market rate of interest, due allowance being made for risk.

3) The prices of all assets are equal to the values of their quasi-rents discounted at the market rate.

Where barriers to entry exist, these propositions hold, if at all, only approximately, the null hypothesis being that high barriers are associated with high rates of return *ceteris paribus*. Or to formalize the rate equalization argument in a partial adjustment model, we may hypothesize that high barriers to entry are associated with low adjustment parameters.

3

Equity Markets and
the Accounting System

The previous chapter established the basis of the well-known rate equalization theorem. All of the necessary ingredients were implicit, but important institutional details were not made explicit. This is done in this chapter. The first section traces the role of equity markets and highlights the need for an accounting system. Some of the issues raised in this section are then developed in detail in the succeeding sections. In particular, the institutional details of the accounting system lead to an hypothesis alternative to barriers to entry explaining lags in rate equalization.

Equity Markets

The Marshallian model developed in the previous chapter concentrated on the role of the entrepreneur. The barrier-to-entry literature followed that emphasis. New firms were created by entrepreneurs who were presumed to actually own the new firms themselves. No mention was made there of the funds they would need to borrow to buy the plant and equipment and pay the wages and salaries necessary to create the productive asset we call a firm. Nor was the role of the investor clearly delineated.

The Fisherian model on the other hand, while explicit about the role of investors in setting the rate of interest and providing funds to an endowment-less firm, assumes that firms are created *ab novo* each period. There is no room in this formulation for second-hand firms.

Both pictures are misleading from a number of points of view, two of which are stressed here. As Tobin and Brainard (1976) point out, a central feature of a capitalist economy is the existence of long-lived second-hand assets side by side with new assets. As noteworthy is the fact that ownership of these second-hand assets is widely spread among investors through equity shares. These two facts have several implications for this study.

First, while the Marshallian model concentrates on the markets for and the production of real commodities, this book is concerned with the interface between these markets and capital markets. Second, while the Fisherian model deals with the return on new firms, this study is primarily concerned with the return on old firms. Equivalently, while investment theory refers for the most part to primary issues in the equity market, i.e., issues of new shares, this study is concerned with the buying and selling of old shares, i.e., in the ongoing secondary market. The relationship of equity markets in existing firms to the theory of the previous chapter is the topic of this chapter.

Note first that I distinguished earlier, in the context of the Fisherian model especially, between real investment and financial investment. Real investment was defined as the accumulation of physical plant and equipment by entrepreneurs. Financial investment was defined as the purchase by investors of already existing plant and equipment. Equivalently, real investment, by the definition used here, involves new firms and new equity, while financial investment involves old equity and second-hand firms.

Clearly these activities are closely related. They do, however, take place in separate markets between which an arbitrage process is assumed to operate. In the case of real investment, physical assets are traded. In the case of financial investment, equities, or the rights to benefits from these physical assets, are traded. In full equilibrium, the ownership of physical assets should yield the same benefits as the equity in those assets, and they will therefore exchange at the same price.

This last is less trivial than it appears at first glance. The owner of equity shares in a firm has no rights *per se* over the physical disposition of the firm. At no stage does the investor take possession of a physical asset. All that the investor is entitled to is a share in the net proceeds generated by the firm. The advantage of this is that ownership of benefits may pass hands continuously without ever disturbing the physical plant itself. And, in fact, equities are traded daily on exchanges throughout the world.

In recent years, considerable evidence has accumulated to show that these equity markets are extremely efficient in the sense that all publicly available information is impounded in the equity price at any given moment in time. Stochastically, this implies that prices follow a random walk. Furthermore, one may conclude from this that prices reflect the market's valuation of the expected future benefits from these equities. Equivalently, the equity market itself moves into equilibrium very rapidly, removing within hours, it would appear, the possibility of earning abnormal profits.

This is true for all firms regardless of their behavior, i.e., allowing for risk, the return earned by an investor on the most poorly managed and inefficient company on the exchange is identical to the return earned by the investor on the best managed and most efficient. To see this formally, using our earlier notation, note that the average return on a productive asset when its net present value W_0 has been capitalized is $q_1/(-q_0 + W_0)$. But by definition, regardless of where q_1 and q_0 are, including inefficient points below the transformation curve, the budget line always holds and it is true that with p_0 as numeraire

$$q_1 = (-1/p_1)q_0 + W_1 \tag{3.1}$$

and since this yields when q_1 is zero that

$$W_1 = W_0(1+r) \tag{3.2}$$

and since by (2.11)

$$(1/p_1) = (1+r) \tag{3.3}$$

it follows that

$$\frac{q_1}{-q_0 + W_0} = \frac{-(1+r)q_0 + W_0(1+r)}{-q_0 + W_0} \tag{3.4}$$

$$= (1+r)$$

In words, the return earned on equity shares in a firm will be the risk-adjusted equilibrium rate regardless of the firm's productive efficiency or of the existence of barriers to entry.

Three things are true, of course. First, the original holder of an equity could hold on to the equity and thereby take the rent in the form of income. It is the published price of the security which is such that no purchaser of the equity can expect to reap this gain. Second, the above is simply an application of the efficient market hypothesis which says that all public information will be impounded in the price of a security so that only a normal return may be expected on that equity. If unexpected information arrives, the price will adjust swiftly by that hypothesis to reflect the new information and again ensure a normal return only. In the process, the holder will obtain an unexpected capital gain or suffer an unexpected capital loss, but short of tallying the day-to-day transactions of every shareholder, there is no way one can calculate the profit being earned. Third, all of the above is also a simple application of equation (2.33), which stated that the return on an asset would adjust so that the return on the asset would equal the market rate of interest—plus, it was suggested, a suitable risk premium.

Two important results emerge from this. First, the theoretical economic picture as portrayed in the last chapter has to be modified to take into consideration institutional details. In the Fisherian model, for instance, it was assumed that each period there is an *ab novo* decision on how much of this period's consumption goods to invest. The decision rule was to invest to the point where the production function was a tangent to the budget line. Where this led to positive net wealth W_0, entrepreneurs or investors were presumed to step in *then* and buy the asset at its present value, thereby eliminating profits from the industry. This, however, puts in two stages what in reality happens side by side in the economy. Real investment is not succeeded by financial investment—they take place simultaneously, i.e., equity shares are traded at the same time as physical plant is accumulated.

Second, and as a result, there is no way to read off from the return being earned by investors on a firm's equity anything about the firm, except perhaps its risk level. Whether the firm has invested to its optimum level, what marginal or average return it is earning on its assets, even whether it is efficient or inefficient is all information that a securities market cannot provide. It is information, however, that is clearly required to ensure efficient allocation of physical resources in the economy and it must therefore be provided by an alternative information system.

Stated in other words, for the partial adjustment equation

$$r_t = r_{ot}^e + \lambda(\varrho_t^e - r_{ot}^e) \tag{3.5}$$

to have meaning, r_t must be defined as something other than a return on equity, i.e., if r_t were to be defined as the return on equity, the adjustment parameter would, by the efficient market hypothesis, always be unity. What we are after, of course, is a return on physical assets, as distinct from the return on assets. Equivalently, we want the return on cost $(-q_0)$, not the return on value $(-q_0 + W_0)$.

The accounting system goes part of the way to fulfilling this need, and the balance of this chapter is devoted to a discussion of accounting rates of return. It is interesting to note that economic theory is almost wholly silent on the role of accounting. Yet without it, there could be no studies of productive efficiency, monopolistic practices, or barriers to entry, since, as we have seen, the equity market discounts all imperfections to yield a normal rate of return at all times.

However, we do need the return on equity because, by assumption of arbitrage or, equivalently, by assumption of the rate equalization theorem, the return on physical assets must continually be tending toward the return on the equity in those physical assets. This arbitrage process occurs as costs tend to values. The speed of this process is governed, Bain would argue, by the height of the barriers to entry in that industry. Were there no barriers to entry, replacement cost would be equal to value at all times, and the return on equity would be equal to the return on physical assets.

The Accounting System

The previous section argued that the return earned by investors on the value of their equity holdings would always be the equilibrium rate, which we shall denote ϱ. This is also the marginal return earned on physical assets when the investment program is complete, i.e., in terms of equation (3.5), when the adjustment parameter equals unity. The barrier-to-entry literature suggests that for various reasons the investment program will be incomplete and firms will find themselves earning a marginal rate of physical assets above that of the long-run equilibrium rate. To demonstrate this it is usual to turn to average rates and to the average accounting rate since, as we have seen, the return on equity is useless for this purpose and marginal returns are simply unavailable.

The accounting system has several important features that bear consideration. First, in general, although there are a few major exceptions, accountants enter assets at cost and not at market value. All costs are in monetary units, of course. The effect is to exclude the present value W_0 of the Fisherian model from the books of the company. Second, except where the cash revenue from sales will only be collected in the relatively distant future, i.e., beyond one period from delivery, sales are entered at face value. Otherwise stated, p_1, the price of goods one period hence, will not enter the books of the company. There is also a lag between the response of the equity market and the accounting system, which is treated in more depth in the section entitled "Plans and Actions," but which we can pass over for the moment. Third, and more obviously, the system provides at best average rates of return. Short of knowing the transformation function, the marginal return on assets cannot be established. Given these few facts, we can draw up the accounts of the Fisherian entrepreneur. The journal entries will be:

dr Assets $-q_0$
   cr Equity $-q_0$

The initial investment where the asset is priced at \$1/unit.

dr Cash q_1
   cr Sales q_1

The sale of the asset produced at the price of \$1/unit holding in period one.

Income Statement:

Sales	q_1
Cost of Sales	$-q_0$
Net Income	$q_1 + q_0$

Opening Balance Sheet:

Assets	$-q_0$	Equity	$-q_0$

Closing Balance Sheet:

Cash	q_1	Equity	$-q_0$
		Retained Earnings	$q_1 + q_0$

For good sense, I calculate the return on the assets in the opening balance sheet rather than on the contemporaneous assets and will use this definition throughout, except where explicitly stated otherwise. To distinguish the accounting rate from the equity rate ϱ and the money rate i, I shall label it r and write

$$r = \frac{q_1 + q_0}{-q_0}$$

$$= q_1/(-q_0) - 1 \tag{3.6}$$

In general (3.6) is not the marginal rate. However, if constant returns to scale obtain it will be. By assumption, these apply in the long run. Thus, we can assume that, in the long run, the accounting rate will tend to the desired marginal rate on physical assets. Otherwise stated, to the extent that supplies are elastic, the accounting rate will approximate the marginal rate. When supplies are relatively inelastic, the two will diverge, and the best one can say is that as the marginal rate decreases as investment increases so the average rate will decrease. Formally, we have

$$r(x) = f(x)/x \tag{3.7}$$

where x = rate of production

$f(x)$ = production function

r = average return

and $f'(x)$ = marginal return

But $f(x) = x \cdot r(x)$ (3.8)

whence $f'(x) = r(x) + x \cdot r'(x)$ (3.9)

If the production function were known, the divergence $x \cdot r'(x)$ could be calculated. In its absence, one is forced to approximate it, say by a constant, which should suffice for small differences around $f'(x)$, i.e., one has very roughly

$$r = \varrho + \alpha$$

where α is a positive constant and a function of the concavity of the production function. This suggests that a constant should be included in the equation (3.5) to give

$$r_t = \alpha + r_{ot}^e + \lambda(\varrho_t^e - r_{ot}^e)$$ (3.10)

We may now interpret r_t as the observed accounting rate and r_{ot}^e as the marginal no-investment rate. Clearly this is unsatisfactory, but there is little else the empiricist can do. It might be added that the problem addressed here seems to have been almost completely ignored by economists using accounting rates as surrogates for the marginal return on physical assets. There is one major exception to the cost rule that needs to be mentioned. When a public corporation buys the equity of another company for cash, it shows this transaction at cost, which now is market value, i.e., the price includes W_0. Consider, for instance, a financial holding company that buys our entrepreneur out. The transaction would enter the books of the holding company as:

dr	Assets	$-q_0$
	Goodwill	W_0
cr	Cash	$-q_0 + W_0$

If we assume that the company prepares consolidated statements, as it should, the following accounts will appear:

Income Statement:

Sales	q_1
Cost of Sales	$-q_0$
Amortization of Goodwill	W_0
	$q_1 + q_0 - W_0$

Opening Balance Sheet:
  Assets $-q_0$
  Goodwill W_0 Equity $-q_0 + W_0$

Closing Balance Sheet:
  Cash q_1 Equity $-q_0 + W_0$
                                             Retained Earnings $q_1 + q_0 - W_0$

Now defining the accounting rate as before we have

$$r = \frac{q_1 + q_0 - W_0}{-q_0 + W_0}$$

$$= \frac{q_1}{-q_0 + W_0} - 1$$

$$= \varrho$$

It will be noted that the assets are entered at their reproduction cost of $1 and that the difference between this and the price paid is shown as goodwill. It will further be noted that the goodwill has been amortized. The effect, in the absence of unexpected information, is to make the accounting rate equal to the market rate—a result which may be compared with (3.4) above.

In one sense, this confirms that accountants are correct in insisting that goodwill be amortized. In another sense, the amortization of goodwill is destructive of information in that it simply ensures that the accounting rate will equal the already known market rate—and as before, this equality will hold regardless of the state of the investment program of the firm.

What emerges is that to the extent that supply is elastic the accounting rate enables one to distinguish the efficient from the inefficient. It does not, however, enable one to distinguish the proportions of physical investment undertaken, since returns are constant. On the other hand, where the transformation function is concave, the accounting rate is not equal to the desired marginal rate. However, to a crude first approximation, it might be possible to add a constant term to the partial adjustment model (3.5), as has been done. Further if we assume that in general firms are underinvested, the two rates will decrease simultaneously, and one may therefore hope for qualitatively similar movements.

Plans and Actions

The preceding section emphasized the time that it takes for physical goods to be produced and contrasted this with the swiftness of response of the securities market. Further insight is obtained if we distinguish between instruction dates, or what I shall often refer to as plans and action dates, or simply actions. As Bliss (1974) has it:

> A decision is made at some moment of time and we wish to describe such decisions. Now two dates attach themselves to a decision, the date at which it is made, here called the *instruction date* and the date at which the actions defining the decisions are to be carried out, here called the *action date*.

By the Efficient Market Hypothesis, the expected impact of a new investment will be reflected in security prices at the *instruction date* (more correctly, at the time planning is made public.) For simplicity, assume that this is coterminous with the instruction date. The actual action should have no effect on security prices whatever except as reality differs significantly from the expectation.

On the other hand, it is the essence of accounting as presently conceived, and I would argue correctly so, that it responds at *action dates* primarily. A new investment enters the books at the time of purchase, *not* at the time of planning. The definition of action dates is, in fact, the subject of the accounting doctrine of income realization.

Since, in general, instruction dates precede action dates, one should expect, even in an otherwise ideal world, adjustments in market prices to lead adjustments in accounting numbers, with the lead time dependent on the time that must elapse between the instruction date and the action date or dates. Furthermore, the market will lead the final equilibrium accounting rate by a lag equal to the time taken from the instruction date to the complete working out of the adjustment process.

If, by way of example, a firm encounters an unexpected, abnormally profitable opportunity, the market will discount this abnormal profit immediately on receipt of the news, taking into account the expected entry of other entrepreneurs to that market in search of abnormal profits. The only party to benefit will be the holder at that time, since any abnormal return can be expected to be arbitraged away immediately. However, the accounting rate of return will not start to move until the "action" begins, and it will not cease moving until the abnormal profits are finally arbitraged away by the entry of new firms, or its own investment program is complete, or the investment programs of other already existing firms in that industry are complete. In brief, there will be a lag between the market and the books and one which can continue for fairly lengthy periods although in reality the effect has already been completely discounted.

Alternatively stated, one can expect movements in the market price to precede in time any changes in profitability as measured by the accounting system. Equally, movements in market rates should precede movements in accounting rates. In other words, the two do not move coterminously as suggested in the last section. When it comes to operationalizing equation (3.10) this lag must and will be taken into consideration.

Linear Filters

In addition to the lags and reasons for lags already enumerated, there is yet another lag in the system induced by the nature of the accounting process. This is probably most easily introduced by means of an example. Consider the net book value of assets at a point in time t, denoted by B_t. This is, in effect, a weighted sum of the costs of the assets purchased at various times over the life of the firm. With A_t representing the cost of the assets purchased in year t, and with w_t representing the weights, we may write

$$B_t = \sum_{s=0}^{\infty} w_s A_{t-s} \tag{3.11}$$

Still by way of example, assume that asset costs have been constant and that suddenly they double. The response of B_t to this step disturbance is easily traced since

$$B_t = A \sum_{s=0}^{\infty} w_s \tag{3.12}$$

$$B_{t+1} = 2w_0 A + A \sum_{s=1}^{\infty} w_s = B_t + w_0 A \tag{3.13}$$

$$B_{t+2} = 2w_0 A + 2w_1 + A \sum_{s=2}^{\infty} w_s = B_t + w_0 A + w_1 A \tag{3.14}$$

and so on. It should be clear that if the life of the asset is n years so that $w_s \geq 0$ for $s \leq 1$ and $w_s = 0$ thereafter, it will take a full n years before book value doubles and thereby fully reflects the doubled costs of the underlying asset purchases.

Formally, we can capture this effect by the use of the concept of filters. More specifically, consider the class of linear filters, which encompasses all the models of earnings behavior that have been posed in the literature to date. We posit an input sequence X_t, say, an output sequence Y_t, say, and a filter intervening between the two—in our case the accounting system or elements of it as in the case of book value above. For this to be a linear filter we assume

a) the filter is time invariant, i.e., if $Y(t)$ is the response to $X(t)$, then we assume that $Y(t+\tau)$ will be the response to $X(t+\tau)$. In effect, this simply says that the weights the filter imposes on the input sequences are independent of time.

b) the filter is linear, i.e., if $X(t) = a_1 X_1(t) + a_2 X_2(t)$ and the response to $X_1(t)$ and $X_2(t)$ individually is $Y_1(t)$ and $Y_2(t)$, respectively, then the response to $X(t)$ will be $Y(t) = a_1 Y_1(t) + a_2 Y_2(t)$.

In the example above the annual capital expenditure forms the input sequence and the book value of the assets the output sequence. The question can then be asked, how will the output sequence respond to a change in the input sequence? What will the output response be to an impulse, a step, a ramp, or a sinusoid in the input? In the example above, an impulse in the input function would generate an n-period-long, albeit declining, response.

The next question is, then, how one should choose the weights to permit the maximum amount of data to be transmitted. This is in the first place not a matter of information economics, but one of data transmission, i.e., it is a technical question. Like all technical questions, though, the *adoption* of a technical solution will depend on its cost-benefit performance, i.e., it becomes a question of information economics.

One can go on to conceive of the accounting system as a series of filters in parallel and sequence. Diagrammatically, one has something like the figure seen below where E_1 and E_2 are economic events and O_1 is the value reported by the system in response to the events. Note, incidentally, the inclusion of a feedback loop.

Figure 3.1.   Accounting as Multi-Filter

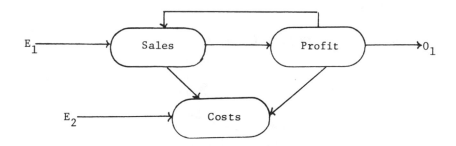

The potential importance of this broader concept is enormous. Manegold (1979), for example, has argued that the stochastic behavior of earnings is a composite of the stochastic behaviors of its various components such as sales and cost of sales. Thus far, all our models have been of the form of a single filter. However, clearly the different subfilters will have different response functions. For instance, revenue can be expected to be extremely responsive to changes in demand. Compare this with the extremely sluggish response of book values of assets. If, therefore, we are to progress in our explanation of accounting rates of return, it is necessary to distinguish both the different causal events that form the input sequence and the subfilters that mediate each class of events. Note that by contrast, it appears that the nature of the disturbance is relatively immaterial in the analysis of the market response. Whether the probability distributions of the investor are affected by changes in revenue or by changes in assets, prices would seem to be of minor interest.

To return to the main task at hand, it should be clear that if quasi-rents do shift upward, accounting income should increase immediately. The response function of growth-adjusted income to a step function in price is itself a step function. One may graph this as follows.

Figure 3.2.   Revenue Response Curve

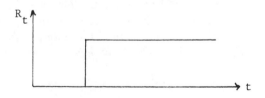

One expects the securities market to adjust security prices almost immediately if this shift is unexpected and in such a way as to return the rate of return to a value consistent with the risk class. One also expects asset prices to change, reflecting the increased quasi-rents. However, even if this latter change occurs almost immediately, the reported book value of the assets of the firm will change only on the *margin*. The response function of book value will look something like this.

Figure 3.3.   Fixed Costs Response Curve

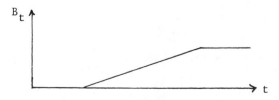

Combining the two it is clear that the accounting rates of return will have a response function of the form.

Figure 3.4. Rate of Return Response Curve

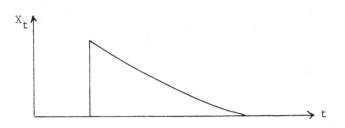

Using the concept of a linear filter and the notation developed earlier, in that context, we can formulate the diagrammatic argument in algebraic terms. We define first the book value of a firm with assets, which originally cost A_t in year t and have an economic life of n years as

$$B_t = \sum_{s=0}^{n-1} w_s A_{t-s} \tag{3.15}$$

Assume for simplicity that the firm is in a stationary state so that A_t is a constant and that the firm uses economic depreciation so that

$$W_0 A = q \sum_{s=1}^{n} v^s \tag{3.16}$$

and

$$w_i A = q \sum_{i+1}^{n} v_s \tag{3.17}$$

where q are quasi-rents, assumed constant, and v is the discount factor. It follows that

$$B_t = q \sum_{s=1}^{n} v_s + q \sum_{s=2}^{n} v^s + \ldots + qv$$

$$= q \{ \frac{v(1 - v^n) + v(1 - v^{n-1}) + \ldots - (1 - v)v}{(1 - v)} \}$$

$$= \frac{q}{\varrho} \{ n - \frac{v(1 - v^n)}{1 - v} \} \quad \text{where } v = (1 + \varrho)^{-1}$$

$$= \frac{nq - A}{\varrho} \tag{3.18}$$

By the same token annual depreciation is

$$D_t = (q - \varrho w_0 A) + (q - \varrho w_1 A) + \ldots + (q - \varrho w_{n-1} A)$$

$$= A \qquad\qquad (3.19)$$

Then it follows that the accounting rate is

$$r = \frac{nq - D}{B}$$

$$= \frac{nq - A}{(nq - A)/\varrho}$$

$$= \varrho \qquad\qquad (3.20)$$

Now assume that at a point $t = 0$ there is a sudden and unexpected rise in all prices of θ. Since this sudden inflation is not expected to continue (by assumption) the rate of interest remains unchanged at ϱ. Now we can write

$$r_1 = \frac{nq(1 + \theta) - A}{(nq - A)/\varrho}$$

$$= \varrho + \frac{\theta\varrho}{1 - A/nq} \qquad\qquad (3.21)$$

Since $(1 - A/nq)$ is always positive, it follows that the accounting rate will rise above the market rate. A year later the most recent asset to enter the books does so at a cost of $(1 + \theta)A$ and depreciation rises by an amount θd_1. As a result

$$r_2 = \frac{nq(1 + \theta) - A - \theta(q - \varrho A)}{(nq - A)/\varrho + \theta A}$$

$$= \varrho + \frac{(n-1)\theta}{n - (1 - \varrho\theta)(A/q)} \cdot \varrho \qquad\qquad (3.22)$$

Since to a first order of magnitude $\varrho\theta$ is negligible we may rewrite this as

$$r_2 = \varrho + \frac{(n-1)\theta}{n - A/q} \cdot \varrho \qquad\qquad (3.23)$$

It follows immediately that

$$r_1 - r_2 = \frac{\theta\varrho}{n - A/q} \tag{3.24}$$

It should be obvious that after n years the accounting rate will have adjusted completely, i.e.,

$$r_1 - r_n = \frac{n\theta\varrho}{n - A/q} \tag{3.25}$$

And it follows immediately that

$$\frac{r_1 - r_2}{r_1 - r_n} = \frac{1}{n} \tag{3.26}$$

To interpret this consider the partial adjustment equation

$$r_t = r_{t-1} + \lambda(\varrho - r_{t-1}) \tag{3.27}$$

Were the adjustment complete in one period, λ would equal one. If no adjustment occurs λ would equal zero. Re-writing this last we have

$$\frac{r_{t-1} - r_t}{r_{t-1} - \varrho} = \lambda \tag{3.28}$$

In other words, comparing (3.26) with (3.28) we see that

$$\lambda = 1/n$$

I have demonstrated that the size of the adjustment parameter in an equation like (3.10) is inversely related to the life of the asset. Moreover, we have an immediate clue as to the potential size of an adjustment parameter; for an asset, whose life is 20 years, it will be on the order of 0.05.

A similar result holds for a growth company. We assume now that the company is growing at a rate of $g = (1 + \Delta)$. The rate before a price change will be ϱ if economic depreciation is being used as before. The rate immediately after a rise in price of θ will be

$$r_1 = \frac{(1+\theta)R_1 - D_1}{B_0}$$

$$= \frac{R_1 - D_1}{B_0} + \frac{\theta R_1}{B_0}$$

$$= \varrho + \frac{\theta R_1}{B_0} \qquad (3.29)$$

The rate a year later will be

$$r_2 = \frac{(1+\theta)gR_1 - gD_1 - \theta g^n(q - \varrho A)}{gB_0 + \theta g^n A}$$

$$= \frac{\varrho B_0 + \varrho \theta g^{n-1}A + \theta R_1 - \theta g^{n-1}q}{B_0 + \theta g^{n-1}A}$$

$$= \varrho + \frac{\theta R_1 - \theta g^{n-1}q}{B_0 + \theta g^{n-1}A}$$

$$\qquad (3.30)$$

To a first approximation we may write this as

$$r_2 = \varrho + \frac{\theta R_1}{B_0} - \frac{\theta q g^{n-1}}{B_0}$$

$$= r_1 - \frac{\theta q g^{n-1}}{B_0} \qquad (3.31)$$

When it follows that

$$\lambda = \frac{r_1 - r_2}{r_1 - \varrho}$$

$$= \frac{q g^{n-1}}{R_1}$$

$$= \frac{q g^{n-1}(g-1)}{q(g^n - 1)} \qquad (3.32)$$

And this to a first approximation yields

$$\lambda = \frac{\{1 + (n-1)\Delta\} \Delta}{\{1 + n\Delta + \frac{1}{2}n(n-1)\Delta^2\} - 1}$$

$$= \frac{1 + (n-1)\Delta}{n + \frac{1}{2}n(n-1)\Delta}$$

$$= \frac{1}{n - \frac{1}{2}n(n-1)\Delta} \tag{3.33}$$

where $(g-1)$ is defined as Δ.

In other words, as one might expect, growth causes the adjustment parameter to increase—without, however, affecting the earlier relationship established with the life of the asset. For example, with growth of 5% and a life of 20 years, the adjustment parameter is of the order of 0.09.

The implication is that although the return on the market value of equity adjusts swiftly, the accounting rate of return will adjust slowly. In contradistinction to the barrier-to-entry-argument, this is a purely accounting-induced phenomenon. If, for example, accountants provided the reproduction cost of assets instead of the historical cost, then any slowness in reversion could be ascribed to investment lags. Given the present institutional arrangements, however, any empirical test of barriers to entry based on accounting rates of return must be severely vitiated by the existence of lags induced by historical costs.

It should be apparent that the speed of reversion will depend on the life of the assets, because the assets are effectively revalued as they are replaced. A new piece of equipment that replaces its older equivalent will enter the books at the current price. The faster this is occurring, the closer the stock of assets will be to current costs. The firm whose assets are turned over within a year will, of course, have them entered at virtually their present replacement cost. In other words, in equation (3.10) one expects the adjustment parameter λ to vary inversely with the life of the assets.

Stated otherwise, the alternative hypothesis of this study is that the apparent observation of adjustment parameters not equal to one is a function of the measurement system instead of economic realities. The argument is that the adjustment process will be heavily influenced by the nature of the filter. Specifically, firms with short-lived assets can be expected to adjust faster than firms with long-lived assets where the life of the asset is defined as the effective book life, and not its actual life, since the different adjustment velocities are being traced here solely to the nature of the filter.

Conclusion

To sum up then, under conditions of perfect competition, all rates within a given risk class will, as we have seen, tend to equality. The argument has been offered that because of structural imperfections in the market, this rate-equalization process will be retarded, leading to excessive profits in industries where high barriers to entry prevail. Translating this in terms of rates, as its proponents do, this suggests an abnormally high rate of return in industries where investment is slow.

To make sense of this argument, it was necessary to use the rates earned on the assets themselves rather than on the equity in those assets. Specifically, the denominator of interest was the replacement cost of the assets. The accounting system as presently constituted does not, however, provide replacement costs, but only the original cost. These tend to current costs as assets are replaced on what we may call the accounting margin. The effect is to induce a lag in the reversion of accounting rates to the appropriate marginal rate involving replacement costs, which is similar to the lag that would be induced by barriers to entry. Hypotheses related to the accounting margin and the investment margin are offered in the following chapter.

4

Maintained, Null, and Alternative Hypotheses

This chapter first outlines the maintained hypotheses that were necessary to build an empirically testable model. Then the null and alternative hypotheses are developed and the proposed tests described.

Maintained Hypothesis

The maintained hypothesis is based essentially on a Marshallian view of the world that may be summarized as follows. Increases in demand cause long-run demand curves to shift to the right and prices to rise accordingly. In the short run supply is fixed. In the longer run existing producers will expand their production in response to the higher prices, while new producers will enter the market. During this process while quantities are slowly adjusting, prices are assumed to adjust swiftly to clear the markets.

To capture this process equation (2.40) was offered, i.e.,

$$r_t = r_{ot}^e + \lambda(\varrho_t^e - r_{ot}^e) + u_t \tag{4.1}$$

This equation contains two unobservable variables ϱ_t^e and r_{ot}^e. To get (4.1) into a form suitable for empirical work, two hypotheses are necessary to convert these variables into observables. The first has already been discussed. It was suggested that the CAPM might enable ϱ_t^e to be modeled, i.e., ϱ_t^e was defined by

$$\varrho_t^e = \alpha + \beta R_{mt}^e \tag{4.2}$$

The sufficient conditions for this model to hold are well known. They are:

1) A perfect capital market in the sense that information is disseminated costlessly and swiftly, enabling arbitrage to take place virtually instantaneously at all times

2) The existence of a riskless, interest-bearing asset

3) Homogeneous beliefs and identical utility functions drawn from a class of linear risk tolerances. Alternatively, heterogeneous beliefs and identical exponential utility functions.

4) Security returns subject to a multivariate normal probability distribution. Alternatively, quadratic utility functions.

All this does, however, is to transfer the problem of expectations from ϱ_t^e to R_{mt}^e since R_{mt}^e is as unobservable as ϱ_t^e. We know, however, that R_{mt}^e is mean reverting (cf. Beaver, 1970), which suggests that an unbiased and efficient estimate of R_{mt}^e is the average of its realizations. Sharpe (1970) reports that the average annual return on the market over the period 1926 to 1965 was 16.5% with a standard deviation of 32.3%. Over the period of this particuliar study the average was closer to 11%.

In a world of no inflation, constant risk, stable capital, and no technological change, this rate would be a constant, Given that none of these factors are constant in the real world, one expects the expected market rate to fluctuate.

This suggests that in place of a constant overall average a moving average should be used that both captures the reverting nature of the process and makes allowances for fluctuations in investor beliefs as risk and inflation expectations change. Logically, the appropriate moving average is a weighted moving average, since this gives the greatest weight to the effect of the most recent information. The point is revisited in the next chapter.

The second problem is to convert the variable r_{ot}^e into an observable variable. Following what appears to be Stigler's intent, this is the accounting rate that would obtain if the firm's physical production remained unchanged, but the increased (decreased) prices engendered by the new opportunity reigned. The variable clearly is intended to reflect the expectations of management. Moreover, given the nature of the market's response, no help can be expected from that quarter. I offer the following, then, as a *first pass* solution.

Assume that the output at time t is q_t, and that a dollar value m_t exists such that with S_t being the common equity of the firm and π_t its profits (the argument is identical with V_t and X_t), we have at time t

$$m_t = \frac{r_t S_t}{q_t}$$

or equivalently

$$r_t = \frac{m_t q_t}{S_t} \tag{4.3}$$

Assume further that management's expectations at time $(t-1)$ of m_t, i.e., m_t^e, are consistent with a simple first-order adaptive expectations model. Then we may write

$$m_t^e = m_{t-1}^e + \delta(m_{t-1} - m_{t-1}^e) \quad \delta \in [0,1] \tag{4.4}$$

which implies

$$m_t^e = \frac{\delta m_{t-1}}{1 - L\gamma}$$

where $\gamma = 1 - \delta$ and L is a lag operator.

We assume further that at time $(t-1)$

$$r_t^e = \frac{m_t^e q_t^e}{S_t^e} \qquad (4.5)$$

but that

$$r_{ot}^e = \frac{m_t^e q_{t-1}}{S_{t-1}} \qquad (4.6)$$

which is consistent with Stigler's argument.

To quote him:

> If it is correctly anticipated that without additional investment the rate of return next year will be 10%, the longrun equilibrium rate being 7%, than an amount of investment may (and, if possible, will) be undertaken that the ex post rate will be only 7 per cent.

Equation (4.5) represents the rate of profit that is expected to obtain given the expected profit per item, i.e., taking into account price changes, the expected quantity that will be purchased, i.e., allowing for expansion or contraction of physical capacity, and the expected equity outstanding, i.e., allowing for equity issues and dividends. Equation (4.6), on the other hand, represents the rate of profit that is expected to obtain if the physical plant, and therefore the physical production and sales, were to remain constant and only the profit margin were to fluctuate. The latter coincides with the no-investment case of Stigler. Substituting, we have

$$r_{ot}^e = \frac{|\delta m_{t-1}|}{1 - L\gamma} \frac{q_{t-1}}{S_{t-1}} = \frac{\delta r_{t-1}}{1 - L\gamma} \qquad (4.7)$$

Before we substitute this back into the model, we need to examine briefly the nature of the δ term here. We note

a) with $\delta = 1 \quad m_t^e = m_{t-1}$

that is, "prices" are assumed to follow a martingale.

b) with $\delta = 0$
$$\begin{aligned} m_t^e &= m_{t-1}^e \\ &= m_{t-2}^e \\ &\cdots \\ &= \mu \end{aligned}$$

that is, "prices" are assumed to be mean-reverting.

Given what we know about security prices, it seems not unreasonable to suspect that δ would be closer to 1 than to 0. This needs to be tempered somewhat by the rather different behavior of product prices, or, at least, observed product prices. Means (1975), for instance, has shown that prices in certain industries are extraordinarily stable. The examination of δ and its effect on the model could, however, constitute a book in itself.

Returning then to our model and substituting for r_{ot}^e, we have

$$\begin{aligned} r_t &= r_{ot}^e + \lambda(\varrho_t^e - r_{ot}^e) \\[1em] &= (1-\lambda)r_{ot}^e + \lambda\varrho_t^e \\[1em] &= \frac{(1-\lambda)\delta r_{t-1}}{1-L\gamma} + \lambda\varrho_t^e \end{aligned}$$

$$r_t - \gamma r_{t-1} = (1-\lambda)\delta r_{t-1} + \lambda\varrho_t^e - \lambda\gamma\varrho_{t-1}^e$$

i.e., $r_t = (1-\lambda\delta)r_{t-1} + \lambda\varrho_t^e - \lambda(1-\delta)\varrho_{t-1}^e$ (4.8)

This may be written as

$$(r_t - r_{t-1}) = \lambda(\varrho_t^e - \varrho_{t-1}^e) - \lambda\delta(r_{t-1} - \varrho_{t-1}^e)$$ (4.9)

which was the form used for later empirical work. The value of δ was deduced from the estimates of $\lambda\delta$ and λ.

It turns out later when estimating the model that r_{ot}^e appears to be misspecified since δ parameters considerably larger than one are encountered. There are several potential reasons for this, each of which indicates how the model might be extended and refined in future research. Essentially they revolve around the fact that an adaptive expectations model is rational only under fairly restrictive conditions. As it stands, the implicit basic assumption is that r_{ot}^e is a constant or that it follows a random walk. A ramp disturbance, for example, leads to biased forecasts using this model. However, if in fact r_{ot}^e is an accounting rate, one factor that management must consider includes just that as a result of steady inflation.

To see what might be happening here, assume that we might have ignored a multiplicative factor F_t—say, for argument's sake only, a cyclical factor. The appropriate formulation would have been

$$\bar{r}_{ot}^{\;e} = \frac{\delta r_{t-1}}{F_{t-1}} + (1-\delta)\,\bar{r}_{ot-1}^{\;e}$$

where

$$\bar{r}_{ot}^{\;e} = \text{the unadjusted expectation}$$

It follows that

$$\bar{r}_{ot}^{\;e} = \frac{\delta r_{t-1}}{(1-\gamma L)\,F_{t-1}}$$

and that

$$r_{ot}^{\;e} = \frac{\delta}{1-\lambda L} \cdot \frac{r_{t-1}F_t}{F_{t-1}}$$

$$= \frac{\delta}{1-\gamma L} x_{t-1} \quad \text{say.}$$

Substituting as before into

$$r_t = \lambda \varrho_t^{\;e} + (1-\lambda) r_{ot}^{\;e}$$

we have

$$r_t - r_{t-1} = \lambda(\varrho_t^{\;e} - \varrho_{t-1}^{\;e}) - \lambda\delta(x_{t-1} - \varrho_{t-1}^{\;e}) - \delta(r_{t-1} - x_{t-1})$$

$$(4.10)$$

To the extent that x_{t-1} differs from r_{t-1} (4.9) is misspecified. If x_{t-1} is greater than r_{t-1} we have an underestimate in the second term in (4.9), and therefore more than likely we will have an overestimate of $\lambda\delta$ and hence of δ. Second-order biases might well also appear in the estimate of λ to the extent that the first and second terms in (4.9) are correlated. These modifications will have to be integrated into future work.

The modifications do not alter the fundamental approach, however. The basic idea is that management calculates the expected, no-investment marginal product of capital and compares it with the expected market rate. The *divergence* between the two indicates whether investment or disinvestment should take place. I believe this to be a wholly accurate view of the fundamental rate equalization process. All that is missing are management's expectations of inflation and of short-run phenomena, such as expected plant utilization. To this must be added, in all good conscience, the effect of accounting changes, which, while not affecting the long-run equilibrium value, do shift the immediate accounting rate onto a different path to that equilibrium rate.

Alternative Hypotheses

Bain and others suggested that the process described above would be impeded by barriers to entry. The argument was also offered that rates of return in industries with strong barriers to entry would be abnormally high. Equation (4.8) has been offered as an operationalized maintained hypothesis and on the basis of this equation it may be hypothesized that in industries where barriers to entry are high the adjustment parameter λ will be relatively small, and vice-versa. In other words, one expects barriers to entry and the adjustment parameters to be negatively correlated, i.e., we may write:

$$H_0: \lambda = \alpha_0 - \beta_0 \times \text{Barriers to entry} \tag{4.11}$$

Since it is possible to derive only ordinal measures of barriers to entry, ordinary linear regression is not possible. A one-way analysis of variance was performed. In other words, the mean value of λ was calculated for each barrier to entry group and the null hypothesis of

$$\overline{\lambda}_1 = \overline{\lambda}_2 = \overline{\lambda}_3 \tag{4.12}$$

was tested.

This is equivalent to an all-dummy variable regression. This latter was performed as well since it yields a little further insight into the relationship of the adjustment parameter to the barrier-to-entry categories. By hypothesis we have

$$\overline{\lambda}_1 < \overline{\lambda}_2 < \overline{\lambda}_3 \tag{4.13}$$

This suggests that if one runs the dummy variable regression equation

$$\lambda = \alpha + \beta_2(0,1,0) + \beta_3(0,0,1) \qquad (4.14)$$

where

$$\hat{\beta}_2 = \bar{\lambda}_2 - \hat{\alpha}$$

and

$$\hat{\beta}_3 = \bar{\lambda}_3 - \hat{\alpha}$$

with

$$\hat{\alpha} = \bar{\lambda}_1$$

we should find both $\hat{\beta}_2$ and $\hat{\beta}_3$ positive.

An alternative test of (4.11) involves the use of the nonparametric Jonkheere test. This assumes ordinal measure only and does a Mann-Whitney count for the three alternatives where $\bar{\lambda}_i < \bar{\lambda}_j$. These counts are summed to create a J statistic, which in the limit is normally distributed. The statistic

$$J^* = \frac{J - \{(N^2 - \sum_{j=1}^{3} n_j^2)/4\}}{\{[N^2(2N+3) - \sum_{j=1}^{3} n_j^2(2n_j+3)]/72\}^{1/2}} = \frac{J-139}{26}$$

is $N(0,1)$ in the limit. These J^* or z values are reported.

The other hypothesis here is that these adjustment parameters are a function of the accounting system. Specifically they are a function of the turnover of assets through the books of the company. The faster the turnover or the longer the effective life of the assets, the smaller would be the value of the adjustment parameter. Formally, we have the hypothesis

$$H_1: \lambda = \alpha_1 - \beta_1 \times \text{Asset life} \qquad (4.15)$$

Since an interval measure of asset life is available, this was tested by a simple linear regression.

The measure of asset life used in this study is the ratio of gross asset value to annual depreciation. To see the reason for this recall that in Chapter 3 I demonstrated that in a no-growth firm

$$\lambda \alpha \frac{1}{N} \tag{4.16}$$

and that in a growth firm to a first approximation

$$\lambda \alpha [n - \tfrac{1}{2}n(n-1)\Delta]^{-1} \tag{4.17}$$

If we assume that the book value of an individual asset can be described by the sequence $\{w_j\}^n_{j=0}$ where $w_0 = 1$ and $w_n = 0$, then we have for the firm as a whole, where the rate of growth is $g = (1+\Delta)$,

$$GB_t = p_0 g^t \sum_{j=0}^{n-1} g^{-j-1}$$

and

$$D_t = p_0 g^t \sum_{j=0}^{n-1} (w_j - w_{j+1}) g^{-j-1}$$

so that our book life as calculated is

$$\frac{GB_t}{D_t} = \frac{\displaystyle\sum_{j=0}^{n-1} g^{-j-1}}{\displaystyle\sum_{j=0}^{n-1} (w_j - w_{j+1}) g^{-j-1}}$$

Where straight line depreciation is used we have

$$w_j = (1 - j/n)$$

so that

$$(w_j - w_{j+1}) = 1/n$$

It follows that

$$\frac{GB_t}{D_t} = \frac{\sum\limits_{j=0}^{n-1} g^{-j-1}}{\frac{1}{n} \sum\limits_{j=0}^{n-1} g^{-j-1}} = n$$

This holds for all rates of growth. Where growth is positive this is, by equation (4.17), an overestimate of the value we want. No adjustment was made for this in this study, which as stated elsewhere is a preliminary investigation only. However, in a minor subsidiary investigation λ was run both against $1/n$ and the growth rate g. If

$$\lambda = \frac{1}{n - t\Delta}$$

and in a regression we set

$$\lambda = \frac{1}{n} + \beta g$$

$$= \frac{1}{n} + \beta(1 + \Delta)$$

then it follows that

$$\beta = \frac{t\Delta}{n(n - t\Delta)(1 + \Delta)}$$

This is clearly positive. The subsidiary investigation revealed a positive regression coefficient as predicted. Since this is only preliminary, no great weight should be placed on this. It is, however, of interest for future research to note that the addition of a growth term appears to strengthen the λ explanations considerably. For example, R-squared's of up to 70% were discovered.

The question that remains is to what extent the two hypotheses overlap. *A priori* it is not unlikely that high barriers to entry may be associated with highly capital-intensive industries. This was, in fact, one of the dimensions both Bain and Mann used to arrive at their classifications. To test this, two regressions were run. The first was to regress lives on barriers to entry. The second was to combine equations (4.14) and (4.15) and to regress the adjustment parameter on both asset life and barriers to entry, i.e., the following equations were run.

$$\text{Asset lives} = \alpha + \beta_2 (0,1,0) + \beta_3 (0,0,1) \tag{4.18}$$

$$\lambda = \alpha + \beta_2(0,1,0) + \beta_3(0,0,1) + \beta_4 \times \text{Asset lives} \tag{4.19}$$

Of course, one of the things we want to ensure is that the rates of profit in the different groups are really different. Thus right at the outset, a one-way analysis of variance was performed on the rates themselves. This was done over the first 8 years, the last 8 years, and all 16 years in the study. It may be noted here that they are indeed significantly different.

A second demonstration of this difference was made using the high-low test found in Beaver (1970). The rates are ranked in year one and split at the median into a high group and a low group. The average rate in each group is calculated and then differenced. These group means and differences are tracked over time. This is repeated beginning in year two and so on. If it is a mean-reverting process one expects the difference to shrink to zero. Beaver (*ibid.*) showed that security rates do indeed revert to the mean very swiftly. However, accounting rates of return revert much more slowly. By the hypothesis of this study, one expects to find a slow rate of reversion among companies with high barriers or long lives. *Pari passu,* one expects to find a faster rate of reversion among companies with low barriers or low lives. Overall, of course, one expects to find a slow rate of reversion as companies maintain their ranks across the three groups.

Prediction

The predictive ability of the model is also of some interest. To evaluate this, the mean square error of prediction of the model was compared with the mean square error of prediction of a simple autoregressive model. This was done in all cases by a one-period-ahead extrapolation and in a number of cases by a random interpolation. To be more precise, a uniform random number generator was used to generate a number from 2 through 17 for each of the 29 companies. The error of prediction was based on calculating the actual minus the estimated value for this randomly chosen year.

Clearly, the autoregressive and model predictions are not independent observations. They are two estimates based on the same body of data. A paired *t*-test was therefore used to test the significance of the difference over the 29 companies. Since the implicit assumption of normality might not be met, a second, nonparametric test was run. This was the Wilcoxon paired sampled test. This test assumes ordinal measure only and essentially counts the number of times the model's mean square error exceeds that of the autoregressive model. For large samples we have for this test,

$$\mu_T = \frac{N(N+1)}{4} = 217.5$$

$$\sigma_T = \frac{N(N+1)(2N+1)}{24} = 46.3$$

$$Z = \frac{T-217.5}{46.3}$$

where T is the Wilcoxon count of differences. These Z values are reported on later.

5

Operationalization and Data Base

The broad intent of the proposed empirical investigation was to estimate the parameters of the adjustment model and to test the associated null hypothesis. This stated that the values of the adjustment parameter would be similar across industries according to Bain's categorizations and that these industry values would be at least qualitatively predictable on the basis of the height of the barrier to entry. The alternative hypothesis suggested that almost all the movement in accounting rates could be attributed to economic adjustments over time as filtered by the accounting system, which obviated the need for explanations based on structural impediments. This chapter discusses the operationalizations needed for the empirical work and the data base used.

Sample Selection

The *basic* constraints on the data were minimal, consisting only of the demand that companies have 12/31 financial year ends to ensure comparability of rates in time, and that they be quoted on the NYSE to ensure the existence of security price data. Banks, Finance, Utilities, Life Insurance, Fire & Casualty, Airlines, REIT's, and Holding companies were excluded either because they are regulated or because they do not report data that are potentially required. This yielded a sample of some 800 companies.

The constraint imposed on the data by the null hypothesis was comparatively severe, however, since it was necessary to rank these companies on the basis of industry barriers to entry. To do this, it was necessary to turn to the work of Bain and Mann. Starting with Bain's sample, it was possible to match about 30 of his 60 companies with my sample—some of his companies had merged, others were privately held, some had disappeared completely, and others were not 12/31 financial year ends. A number of his industries were poorly represented in the COMPUSTAT sample. The associated companies were accordingly discarded. The following 16 companies were left from this winnowing process. (The Roman numerals here and elsewhere indicate the height of the barrier to entry, I being the highest and III being the lowest.)

> Group I:
>   Automobiles
>   General Motors
>   Chrysler

Cigarettes
American Brands—now American Industries
Ligget & Myers
Reynolds Tobacco—now Reynolds Industries
Philip Morris

Group II:
Copper
Anaconda
Kennecott
Phelps-Dodge
Steel
United States
Bethlehem
Republic
Metal Containers
American Can
Continental Can

Group III:
Cement
Lehigh Portland
Lone Star

Mann's later study extended the Bain sample by some 13 industries. He dropped Metal Containers to category III and moved Cement up to category II. His study enabled the sample to be extended to include a further 11 companies, namely:

Group I:
Ethical Drugs
Merck
Pfizer
Schering
Abbott
Automobiles
Ford

Group II:
Cement
Ideal
General Portland

Group III:
  Glass Containers
    Owens-Illinois
    Anchor-Hocking
  Textiles
    Cone
    Dan River

This gave 11 companies in group I spread over 3 industries, 10 companies in category II spread over 3 industries, but only 6 companies in group III spread over essentially 2 industries. It was not possible to match any of Mann's coal companies, which fell into this category, so two were selected from the COMPUSTAT sample to increase the size of this last category. These were

  Eastern Gas & Coal
  Pittston

These 29 companies constituted the sample for testing. There is no pretense that this sample is representative of the market. Bain selected his industries purely on the basis of data availability, as did Mann. They intended the companies selected in each industry to be the dominant firms; thus they do not necessarily reflect the behavior of smaller companies in the same industry.

These companies were selected for *this* study because they are supposed to represent a wide range of barrier-to-entry heights. If the Bain/Mann hypothesis is able to discriminate at all, one expects *a priori* to find different adjustment factors across these industries and, of course, similar adjustment factors within each industry. In short, the hypothesis was that adjustment factors would vary systematically with barriers to entry and the sample was chosen to test this hypothesis.

The Model

In earlier chapters, I argued that the rate equalization process could be captured by the partial adjustment model

$$r_t = r_{ot}^e + \lambda(\varrho_t^e - r_{ot}^e) \qquad (5.1)$$

The left-hand variable r_t is the only observable *ex post* variable in the formulation, which necessitated a series of further assumptions to arrive at an operational model wholly in observed variables. This was done and the equation suggested for empirical purposes was

$$r_t = (1 - \lambda\delta)r_{t-1} + \lambda\varrho_t^e - \lambda(1-\delta)\varrho_{t-1}^e \qquad (5.2)$$

where

$$\varrho_t^e = \alpha + R_{mt}^e \tag{5.3}$$

Since there are only two parameters λ and δ in the model and three predetermined variables, the model was put into a differenced form for estimation purposes, i.e.,

$$(r_t - r_{t-1}) = \lambda(\varrho_t^e - \varrho_{t-1}^e) - \lambda\delta(r_{t-1} - \varrho_{t-1}^e) \tag{5.4}$$

This model was estimated for each of the 29 companies in the sample over 15 years of data and used to calculate a one-year-ahead prediction.

In the sections below, a surrogate for the expected market rate is first discussed. This is followed by a discussion of the characteristics of the accounting rate. These two sections then flow in the next chapter into a discussion of the estimation of the model (5.4) which is followed by the results of the testing of the various hypotheses. The predictive power of the models is discussed.

The Market Return

The first variable that had to be operationalized was the expected market rate of return for the firm, i.e., ϱ_t^e. Since the accounting rate of return covered a period of one year, it was necessary to calculate an annual expected market rate. The first problem one encountered is over what year this rate is to be calculated.

An argument can be made that investors respond to plans rather than to actions, with the implication that reported accounting income is not information, except where the divergence of observed from expected is so great as to revise prior beliefs. Income is, in general, merely confirmation. In the ideal world of period analysis, one can conceive of plans being formulated at the start of a period and the details being disclosed to investors who form their expectations as to the range of probable outcomes. The interaction of these investors in the marketplace leads to an expected rate of return for that period (here a year). This rate is the equity cost of capital and forms the signal to management with respect to their investment plans for that year. All this, of course, is presumed to happen simultaneously and lead ultimately to a temporary equilibrium, where each investor has equalized his expected marginal utility across his margin and management has maximized the expected profit of the firm.

This suggests that, as a first pass, one wants the expected rate in the year before the financial year end. An alternative is the rate in the year before publication of the annual report. This would, on average, shift the calculations roughly three months forward in time. Other lags may also be used. Given that information as to plans is emerging continuously, as opposed to the discrete, once-a-year simplicity of the economic model, the ultimate choice is an empirical one and theoretically arbitrary. For simplicity, the lag corresponding to the financial year end was used. Specifically the annual rate $R12$ was defined by

$$R12 = (1 + RJ)(1 + RF)(1 + RM) \ldots (1 + RD) - 1 \qquad (5.5)$$

where

$RJ =$ the rate for the month of January prior to the financial year end of 12/31

$RF =$ the rate for the month of February, etc.

The annual rate referred to here is the rate of return earned by investors in the equity of the company. It may be denoted R_j or ϱ_j. Against this may be set the average return R_m that would be earned by an investor who invested in all equity securities available. This is generally surrogated by the return on all NYSE firms. Then using the CAPM we have the well-known relationship in (5.3) above.

Recalling that we want an annulized R_j several operational possibilities offer themselves here. One is to take the monthly R_j's as given and substitute directly into (5.5). Another is to run the regression implicit in (5.3) and use the derived $\hat{\alpha}$ and $\hat{\beta}$ to calculate a monthly $\hat{R}_j$ which is then substituted in (5.5). A third is to use (5.5) to arrive at an annualized R_m and R_j and then to calculate an estimated $\hat{R}_j$ from an $\hat{\alpha}$ and $\hat{\beta}$ derived from a (5.3) regression run using the annualized data.

The annual and monthly betas appear in Table 5.8. These are low. This is not entirely unexpected since the 29 companies used in this study make no pretense to be a cross section of the market. They are the dominant companies in a few selected industries and may be expected to be low-risk companies.

The more usual monthly betas were also computed and the results are also shown in Table 5.8. They are marginally higher, but not significantly so, and the rank order is maintained quite well. The Spearman rank correlation coefficient is 0.58 and significant at 0.001. Since it can be argued that monthly betas are more reliable statistically and given that there was little in it, the monthly betas were used in later work.

Two further points were of concern. The first revolves around the formulation of the CAPM and its subsequent estimation using the market model. This concern is basically that the generating model involves both the market rate and the riskless rate, but the estimating model used involved only the market rate. A minor Monte Carlo simulation was therefore done to test the potential bias introduced. To be specific, the 30-day commercial paper rate was aggregated over 12 months to yield an annual rate consistent with the annual market rate. The i.i.d. residual terms were assumed to be normally distributed with a mean of zero and variances of 0.0625, which was the approximate squared standard error of the beta regressions. The individual company rates were then generated for betas from 0.6 through 1.4 in steps of 0.2 using the model

$$R_{jt} = (1 - \beta_j)R_{ft} + \beta_j R_{mt} + u_t \qquad (5.6)$$

The excess return form of this model, i.e.,

$$(R_{jt} - R_{ft}) = \alpha_j + \beta_j(R_{mt} - R_{ft}) + u_t \qquad (5.7)$$

and the model

$$R_{jt} = \alpha_j{}' + \beta_j R_{mt} + u_t \qquad (5.8)$$

were then run on the simulated data sets. The results are shown in Table 5.1.

Table 5.1. (a) Model (5.8)

α	β	R^2	D
0.0047	0.5895	0.41	1.98
−0.0170	0.8017	0.58	1.95
−0.0043	1.0048	0.68	2.02
−0.0200	1.1839	0.78	2.17
−0.0013	1.3979	0.78	2.04

Table 5.1. (b) Model (5.9).

α'	β	R^2	D
−0.0022	0.6045	0.30	2.00
0.0022	0.8145	0.43	1.99
0.0009	0.9832	0.53	2.05
−0.0152	1.1932	0.61	1.98
−0.0158	1.4052	0.68	2.07

The results are encouraging in that no systematic bias in the estimate of betas seems to appear when using the simpler model. The reason is not hard to find. Consider the two models:

$$R_j = (1 - \beta_j)R_f + \beta_j R_m + \varepsilon \tag{5.9}$$

and

$$R_j = a + b_j R_m + \varepsilon \tag{5.10}$$

From (5.10)

$$E(b_j) = E\left[\frac{\Sigma(R_m - \bar{R}_m)(R_j - \bar{R}_j)}{\Sigma(R_m - \bar{R}_m)^2}\right]$$

From (5.9)

$$(R_j - \bar{R}_j) = (1 - \beta_j)(R_f - \bar{R}_f) + \beta_j(R_m - \bar{R}_m) + (\varepsilon - \bar{\varepsilon})$$

We have, after substituting, and some fairly trivial rearrangements,

$$E(b_j) = (1 - \beta_j)\sigma_{mf}\frac{\sigma_f}{\sigma_m} + \beta_j$$

where

$$\sigma_{mf} = \text{Covariance of } R_m \text{ and } R_f$$

$$\sigma_m^2 = \text{Variance of } R_m$$

$$\sigma_f^2 = \text{Variance of } R_f$$

Clearly

$$\sigma_f << \sigma_m$$

so that

$$E(b_j) \approx \beta_j$$

The two expected values will be close, given the variance ratio. Therefore, I have continued to use the simpler model in estimating betas.

The second point of concern was whether R_m accounts for all the cross-sectional variation in the market, specifically whether $o(u_{it}, u_{jt}) = 0$. Little or nothing can be done about the existence of cross-sectional variation in the estimation of the CAPM itself when it exists. However, cross-sectional variation carries through into the model (5.2) where, because r_{t-1} differs from company to company, it *is* possible to gain extra efficiency using the Zellner technique of seemingly unrelated regressions.

To test the assumption cross-sectional correlations of the residuals from the 17-year monthly regressions were calculated. Some of the results are reported in Table 5.9. The correlations are significantly positive throughout, suggesting that the Zellner technique might offer an attractive estimation alternative for the model.

These correlations also shed light on Bain's groups and on industries generally. It is apparent that the correlation of the company with its group mean is consistently higher than with the overall mean. This is partly spurious, however, since the company is included in the mean and has a proportionately greater effect in the group mean than in the overall mean. To gauge this effect define

$$S_n = \sum_1^{n-1} X_n$$

and

$$A_n = S_n/n$$

When the desired "true" correlation is

$$\varrho^* = \frac{\text{cov}(X_n, A_{n-1})}{o(X_n)\, o(A_{n-1})} = \frac{\text{cov}(X_n, S_{n-1})}{o(X_n)\, o(S_{n-1})} \tag{5.11}$$

By the same token the correlation, as calculated, is

$$\varrho = \frac{\text{cov}(X_n, S_n)}{o(X_n)\, o(S_n)}$$
$$= \varrho^* \frac{(S_{n-1})}{(S_n)} + \frac{(X_n)}{(S_n)} \tag{5.12}$$

But

$$\sigma^2(S_n) \approx n\sigma^2(X_n) + 2n\sigma^2(X_n)\,\varrho(X_t, X_s) \tag{5.13}$$

Since these latter correlations are of the order of 0.5, one has as a further approximation

$$\sigma^2(S_n) = 2n\sigma^2(X_n) \tag{5.14}$$

and hence

$$\varrho = \varrho^*\sqrt{(n-1/n)} + 1/\sqrt{(2n)} \tag{5.15}$$

With n equal to 29, we have for the overall mean

$$\varrho^* = 1.02\varrho - 0.13 \tag{5.16}$$

With n equal to 10 we have for the group means

$$\varrho^* = 1.05\varrho - 0.23 \tag{5.17}$$

An overall calculated mean of 0.4, say, implies a true mean of 0.28 and a group mean of 0.6, say, a true mean of 0.4. A difference, therefore, remains, albeit an attenuated one. This suggests that there might be group or industry effects present.

This last is consistent with the results of Morgan (1975), Hamada (1972), and King (1966), who found industry effects in the market. For instance, by aggregating companies into six-company industry portfolios, Morgan was able to produce a wide spectrum of betas. Hamada also found betas differing significantly across industries. Specifically he found betas for

Food & Kindred	0.815
Chemicals & Allied	0.928
Petroleum & Coal	0.747
Primary Metals	1.399

In turn, King used factor analysis to demonstrate an industry effect additional to that of the market effect. Since several of his companies overlap with this study, some of his results are presented below. The four periods referred to are 1) 1927-1935; 2) 1935-1944; 3) 1944-1952; and 4) 1952-1960.

Table 5.3 demonstrates how the variance explained by the market factor has declined over the years. The first line for each company is the proportion of variance R_{jt} explained by the first centroid factor and the second the proportion explained by the first principal factor.

Table 5.2.   Percentage of Security Variance Explained by Market

Periods	1	2	3	4	Overall
Ligget & Myers (LM)	.61	.30	.23	.13	.43
	.62	.28	.21	.11	.43
Philip Morris (PM)	.25	.41	.23	.15	.26
	.24	.38	.20	.14	.26
Reynolds (REYN.)	.59	.42	.30	.08	.39
	.60	.37	.29	.07	.38
Bethlehem (BETH.)	.74	.63	.59	.62	.68
	.74	.69	.62	.68	.70
Republic (REP.)	.84	.69	.55	.56	.75
	.84	.75	.56	.61	.77
U.S. Steel (U.S.)	.68	.70	.67	.58	.66
	.69	.76	.69	.64	.68

Two factors stand out. One is the tremendous decline in the explanation of the market factor—overall it dropped from 52% to 31%. The other is the maverick behavior of Philip Morris, which occurs again and again. For instance, it appears again in Table 5.3, which shows the percentage of variance explained by regressing the return of each company on the returns of the remaining 62 companies in his sample.

Table 5.3.   Percentage of Security Variance Explained by Sample

Periods	1	2	3	4	Overall
LM	.93	.89	.84	.88	.76
PM	.40	.84	.73	.88	.45
REYN.	.91	.89	.85	.77	.67
BETH.	.94	.95	.92	.94	.87
REP.	.95	.97	.90	.92	.88
U.S.	.95	.07	.94	.91	.85

He also presents factor loadings on the market $F1$ and the two industries $F2$ and $F4$, respectively, as well as the other industries in his sample. They appear as follows.

Table 5.4. Factor Loadings on Industries

Factors	1	2	3	4	5	6	7
LM	.04	.03	− .00	.00	− .00	− .00	− .00
PM	.04	.02	.00	.00	− .00	− .01	.00
REYN.	.04	.02	− .00	.00	− .00	.00	− .00
BETH.	.10	− .01	− .00	.04	− .00	.00	.00
REP.	.13	− .00	.00	.04	− .00	.00	.00
U.S.	.08	− .00	− .00	.03	.00	.00	.00

Philip Morris is now in line with the others, but the cigarettes stand out as a whole, with a much higher relative loading on the industry factor. That tobacco and metal industries differ sharply is confirmed by the negative industry correlations drawn from his table.

Table 5.5. Correlation of Tobacco and Metal Industry Returns

Periods	1	2	3	4	Overall
Tobacco vs. Metals	− .083	− .524	− .391	− .367	− .359

These results are difficult to interpret. Anyone familiar with industry classifications will know that they coincide only by a very large stretch of the imagination with any economic concept of a market. For instance, sanitary napkins and paper diapers find themselves in the same four-digit classification (SIC 2647), although they constitute no competition for one another. On the other hand, plastic gutters and metal gutters find themselves in separate *two*-digit classifications (SIC 3097 and SIC 3444), despite being almost perfect substitutes for one another. R.J. Reynolds, classified as a tobacco company, now draws some 40% of its income from a Middle Eastern crude oil producer subsidiary, Aminoil. Almost half of the copper company Kennecott's profits at one point were being derived from a coal subsidiary, Peabody—and so on.

The difference in accounting rates might be attributed to industry accounting practices and to the way the accounting system filters changes in asset prices. However, this does not explain the differences in market rates and market betas. However, for whatever reason, the variance explained by an industry factor varies substantially across industries and has increased significantly over time.

To summarize the discussion up to this point, both "monthly" and "annual" betas were derived for each company by regressing the company rates against the market average. In the case of the annual beta the rates used were the geometric averages of the 12 monthly rates in the year before the financial year end, e.g., for a financial year end 12/31, the months January, February, through December were used. What remained was to arrive at an estimate of the expected return on the security over that year.

There is surprisingly little discussion of this point in the literature. In part this is because there is not much that one can say with any confidence. Expectations are notoriously difficult to quantify. Muth (1961), following on earlier suggestions by Modigliani and Grunberg (1954), suggested that economic models should assume that expectations are rational in the sense that the actors make use of the known stochastic properties of the series under consideration.

It is well known from Beaver (1970) that rates of return display pure mean-reverting properties. These were relied upon to arrive at an estimate of $E(R_m)$. Since the individual securities display the same stochastic properties it is possible to arrive at an estimate of $E(R_j)$ directly. Beaver (ibid.) showed that this behaves consistently with the equation

$$R_t^e = \mu + u_t \quad \text{where } Eu_t = 0 \text{ and } u_t \text{ is i.i.d.} \tag{5.18}$$

He showed that the serial correlation of first differences of a sample of NYSE-COMPUSTAT firms was -0.46, which is close to the theoretical value of -0.50 one would expect from a mean-reverting process. The original series showed a serial correlation of close to zero which again is the value one would expect from a mean-reverting process.

In a world of no inflation, constant risk, stable capital, and no technological change this rate would be constant. Given that none of these factors is constant in the real world, one expects the expected market to fluctuate. This suggests that in place of a constant, an overall moving average should be used, which both captures the mean-reverting nature of the process and makes allowance for fluctuations in investors' beliefs as risk and inflation expectations change. Logically, the appropriate moving average is a weighted moving average since this gives the greatest weight to the effect of the most recent information. Of course, should the underlying rate indeed be a constant, the weighted moving average will give the same value as the ordinary moving average. Alternatively, one can reformulate (5.18) slightly to give

$$R_t = \mu + u_t - \theta u_{t-1} \tag{5.19}$$

when

$$R_t^e = \mu - \theta u_{t-1}$$

$$= \mu - \theta(R_{t-1} - R_{t-1}^e) \tag{5.20}$$

This remains perfectly consistent with the fair-game theory of security price behavior, which states that if

$$X_{j,\ t+1} = p_{j,\ t+1} - E(p_{j,\ t+1}|\phi_t) \tag{5.21}$$

then

$$E(x_{j,\ t+1}|\phi_t) = 0 \tag{5.22}$$

when $p_{j,\ t+1}$ is the price of the security at time $(t+1)$ and ϕ_t is the information impounded in past security prices.

Restating this in return form, the definition of a fair game is that if

$$z_{j,\ t+1} = R_{j,\ t+1} - E(R_{j,\ t+1}|\phi_t) \tag{5.23}$$

then

$$E(Z_{j,\ t+1}|\phi_t) = 0 \tag{5.24}$$

But, by the assumptions of (5.19)

$$R_{j,\ t} = \mu + u_t - \theta u_{t-1} \tag{5.25}$$

and

$$E(R_{j,\ t}|\phi_t) = \mu - \theta u_{t-1} \tag{5.26}$$

so that

$$Z_{j,\ t} = u_t \tag{5.27}$$

when

$$E(Z_{j,\ t}|\theta_{t-1}) = 0 \tag{5.28}$$

The advantage of (5.19) over (5.18) is twofold. First, it gives some insight into why Beaver and others might have obtained first-order serial correlations that were not exactly zero and first-order, first-difference serial correlations that were not exactly -0.5. This follows since

$$E(\Delta R_t^2) = E(u_t - \theta u_{t-1} - u_{t-1} + \theta u_{t-2})^2$$

$$= 2(1 + \theta + \theta^2)\sigma^2 \tag{5.29}$$

Also

$$E(\Delta R_t \Delta R_{t-1}) = E(u_t - \theta u_{t-1} - u_{t-1} + \theta u_{t-2})$$

$$(u_{t-1} - \theta u_{t-2} + \theta u_{t-3})$$

$$= -(1 + 2\theta + \theta^2)\sigma^2 \tag{5.30}$$

so that the first-order, first-difference serial correlation is

$$= -\frac{1}{2} \cdot \frac{1 + \theta + \theta^2}{1 + 2\theta + \theta^2} \tag{5.31}$$

which is -0.5 only when θ is zero and is slightly below -0.5 in absolute terms when θ is small positive. Beaver reports a mean value of -0.46.

Similarly, the ordinary first-order serial correlation coefficient is given by

$$E(R_t^2) = E(u_t - \theta u_{t-1})^2$$

$$= (1 + \theta^2)\sigma^2 \tag{5.32}$$

$$E(R_t R_{t-1}) = E(u_t - \theta u_{t-1})(u_{t-1} - \theta u_{t-2})$$

$$= -\theta\sigma^2 \tag{5.33}$$

yielding a coefficient of

$$-\frac{\theta}{+1 + \theta^2} \tag{5.34}$$

This will be small negative for θ small positive. Beaver reports a mean value of -0.11 which yields a θ of roughly 0.11. This yields a first-order, first-difference serial correlation coefficient of -0.47, which is consistent with Beaver's results.

The second advantage of this formulation is that it suggests how an expected value for a security might be derived. This is purely and simply

$$R_t^e = \bar{R}_{t-1} + \theta(R_{t-1} - R_{t-1}^e) \qquad (5.35)$$

where

$$\bar{R}_{t-1} = \frac{1}{n} \sum_{s=0}^{n-1} R_{t-s} \qquad (5.36)$$

This may be demonstrated to minimize the mean square error of prediction.

It remains to chose a value for the parameter θ. This must clearly be small given the values reported by Beaver. The value empirically determined was a mean of 0.4. This is higher than Beaver's results indicate, but a value lower than this reduces the explanatory power of the model considerably. A run was also made with adjusted values of θ to cope with the varying volatility of securities. The argument is that the more volatile a stock is, the more likely an observer is to place weight on previous prediction errors, i.e., to take the last observation into account. Similarly, the less volatile, the more weight the observer will place on the long-run average. Thus the weights used in this run were 0.4β.

The results from this formulation were not entirely satisfactory. An exponentially weighted average model was therefore also tried. In one sense, this is the opposite end of the spectrum from the pure mean-reversion model, since it assumes that the expected value changes from period to period. In another sense, it is merely another formulation of a moving-average model. To motivate it we assume

$$R_t = R_{t-1} + u_t - \theta u_{t-1} \qquad (5.37)$$

so that

$$R_t^e = R_{t-1} - \theta u_{t-1} \qquad (5.38)$$

and

$$u_{t-1} = R_{t-1} - R_{t-1}^e \qquad (5.39)$$

whence

$$R_t^e = R_{t-1} - \theta(R_{t-1} - R_{t-1}^e)$$

$$= \theta R_{t-1}^e + (1-\theta)R_{t-1} \qquad (5.40)$$

This can also be written as

$$R_t^e = (1-\theta) \sum_{s=0}^{\infty} \theta^s R_{t-s+1} \qquad (5.41)$$

in which form it is apparent that our estimate of R_t^e is simply another version of a weighted moving-average model. It is, of course, also consistent with a fair-game model since

$$E(R_{j,\,t}|\phi_{t-1}) = R_{j,\,t-1} - \theta u_{t-1} \qquad (5.42)$$

and therefore

$$Z_{j,\,t} = u_t \qquad (5.43)$$

whence

$$E(Z_{j,\,t}|\phi_{t-1}) = 0 \qquad (5.44)$$

This model was run with parameters of 0.4 and 0.6 with very little difference in the results—both were equally poor. It was found that by setting the parameter to $\beta\theta$ the results improved somewhat. The justification, as before, is that this makes allowance for varying degrees of volatility. Clearly, however, this needs further investigation in future research.

It was suggested earlier that a weighted average would be appropriate. This would be combined with the betas as calculated above to give an expected security rate in accordance with the formula (5.3) above. An alternative and preferable method suggests itself, however. First, the procedure as outlined yields an estimated beta coefficient and not the true beta coefficient, inducing an errors-in-variables problem into the model estimation. Second, the security rate is as mean-reverting as the market rate. Instead, therefore, of going through this two-step procedure, a direct weighted average of the security rate was calculated and used except where otherwise indicated. Since the security rates have varying volatilities, which induces bias into the estimating procedure, the weighted average factors used were proportional to the betas calculated above.

The Accounting Rate

Various alternative definitions of an accounting rate of return present themselves to the researcher. Some of these are discussed below.

1) One can, for instance, follow Stigler and others and calculate a return on total assets, which includes interest and profit in the numerator, or one can follow many others and use the simpler return on equity or common stock. Since the expected market rate was defined as the security market rate, the latter definition seemed to be more appropriate.

2) One can also exclude extraordinaries or include them. This is more of a problem in the earlier years where firms had more discretion in their reporting practices. However, since APB Opinion 9, 1967, extraordinaries have been infrequent and limited largely to disposals of subsidiaries at a loss. A scan of the data showed that the few extraordinaries in this sample were insignificant and the decision was made to exclude them.

3) One can exclude income from unconsolidated subsidiaries and temporary investments, as Stigler did, or include it as did this study. Exclusion may make sense when the company has a dominant, well-defined activity and relatively small, very diverse subsidiaries. However, with the enormous diversification of recent years, exclusion appears arbitrary and less meaningful, and it can be argued that one should be looking at the return on the company as a whole, which includes investment income.

4) There is also a matter of timing. Some researchers use end-of-year income and start-of-year book. Others use an average book figure in the denominator. Still others use end-of-year income over end-of-year book. The end-of-year book was the formulation used in this study, except where indicated to the contrary.

5) COMPUSTAT provides two equity figures—items 11 and 60. The latter is equity as reported by the company in the balance sheet. The former purports to be "real" equity in the sense that it excludes intangibles and the difference between the liquidating value of preferred stock and its carrying value. Common equity as reported was the desired figure. Unfortunately, this is not disclosed on the tapes in the early years when only the "real" figure was given. COMPUSTAT still does not report the carrying figure for preferred stock—it shows only the liquidating value and its redemption value. One is therefore unable to work back to the equity as reported figure. Two options are available to calculate the equivalent figure—excluding or including preferreds.

Both methods were tried and compared with equity as reported, when available. An eyeball scan suggested that the difference was on the average immaterial, although differences in selected cases can be substantial, and that the second definition seemed on balance to be closer. This was, therefore, the denominator used when the desired denominator was not available. The rates affected are all within the first five years of the study and are not expected to have any significant impact whatsoever. Apart from reporting the fact it is a total non-issue.

The COMPUSTAT tape used runs from 1956 through 1975 with most of 1975 not available. Since several of the companies do not appear on the CRSP tape until after 1956, the decision was made to use the 17 years of data from 1958 through 1974. The model has a lag of one year, so this provides 16 years of data effectively. The last year was subsequently reserved for predictive purposes so that ultimately the model was run over 15 data points.

This might seem inadequate. However, some of the basic premises of this study should be borne in mind. One of them is that the generating process is essentially nonstationary. In other words, the behavior of U.S. Steel at the turn of the century is of less interest in explaining its behavior now. Moreover, the thrust of this study is toward using even fewer data points—longitudinally, that is. The aim is to eventually move to cross-sectional pooling where the number of companies used will make up for the shortness of the time series used. Add to that the already demonstrated "naive" nature of the accounting return series and it is clear that 15 data points might be adequate.

The average accounting rates for the companies used are shown in Table 5.10 for the years 1958/65, 1966/73, and 1958/73. Alongside these are the average rates, where available, of the same companies as calculated by Bain and Mann for the periods 1936/40, 1947/51, and 1950/60. The industry averages shown are those calculated by the respective authors over their samples and do not coincide with a simple average of the companies shown. This is not a significant factor, however, provided one accepts the notion of an industry. The samples do, in any case, overlap to a considerable degree.

It is abundantly clear from this table that differences do exist between industries and that these differences have been stable over a considerable period of time. A one-way analysis of variance over the industries for the three periods reveals significant differences.

Table 5.6.　ANOVA on Industry Returns: All Groups

Period	F Value	Significance
1958/73	4.4	0.003
1958/65	3.5	0.011
1966/73	5.0	0.002

Group I, which represents high-barrier-to-entry companies, is seen to have a mean that is substantially above the other two groups, which are much closer to one another. This is consistent with the work of Bain and Mann. An analysis of variance of Group I against Group II and Group III combined showed highly significant F values.

Table 5.7. ANOVA on Industry Returns: Groups II and III Combined

Period	F Value	Significance
1958/73	19.2	<0.001
1958/65	20.5	<0.001
1966/73	16.3	<0.001

In brief, it is patent that there are substantial differences among the companies and industries and that these differences have persisted over a remarkably long period of time. Bain and Mann attribute this to barriers to entry. This study hypothesizes that this is better explained by the normal working of the competitive process as filtered by the accounting system.

These results are further confirmed by the results of high-low tests, which are reported in Table 5.12. A description of the test may be found in Chapter 4. The groups run were Category I, II, and III, Category II and III combined, and Category I, II, and III combined. The hope was that the test would reveal differential reversion across the groups, i.e., high barriers to entry would revert more slowly than low barriers to entry. The results are

Percentage Reversion (by year)	I	II	III	II & III	I, II, & III
8	56	53	64	50	69
1	79	89	75	85	84
Minimum Point					
Year	8	7	16	16	16
%	55	36	49	46	63

Nothing statistically significant emerges from these numbers, which seems to indicate that the rate of reversion is not a function of barriers to entry. There appears, however, to be a concertina effect after about 6 or 7 years in all the groups. The reason for this is not apparent, but when tracked down in future research might affect the tentative conclusion drawn here.

Several factors are worth noting in passing. Bain classified the cement industry in Group III. This study followed Mann in reclassifying these companies into Group II on what were purported to be *a priori* grounds. The subsequent return of the cement industry's rates to its earlier level suggests (*a posteriori*, of course) that the reclassification was perhaps incorrect. Similarly, the steel industry *seems* to be misclassified. It is, however, a well-known fact that domestic steel has suffered severe competition from foreign steel over the past two decades. Rising wages abroad have raised the prices of foreign steel in line with that of domestic steel in recent years, resulting in a return to more normal rates of return. It could be argued that this industry alone and the few figures shown here are "proof" of the rate-equalization process at work on an international scale.

To gain further insight into the data, a few graphs were prepared plotting the accounting rate against time over the period being studied. These are found in Figures (5.1) through (5.3). Each graph is of one industry. The next section discusses one of these industries—the tobacco industry.

The point that emerges from this discussion is that knowledge of the specific situation of each company might enable one to predict fairly accurately what its rate will do in the year ahead. There is, however, no general pattern that is immediately obvious. Regressing across all companies, the likelihood of a "random" model performing well is obviously great. But this does not prove that rates are random. It merely suggests that to explain their movement, one has to get down to some pretty specific modeling. One expects that the market, in the shape of security analysts, is doing just that and, as we shall see later, outperforms a "random" model significantly. The value for theory of modeling the specifics is not, however, clear. It will be shown later that there do appear to be some significant influences at work driving earnings. These are interesting and may contribute to the theoretical literature.

Appendix

The cigarette/tobacco industry is a fascinating example of how swiftly large American corporations can move to protect their positions. The accompanying table is so dramatic that it speaks for itself. For instance, in less than a decade Ligget & Myers shifted its reliance on earnings from tobacco products from 90% to 39%. The reversal that followed was due in part to price controls at a time of sharply increasing raw material prices, which appears to be working itself out again. American Brands, not so long ago known as American Tobacco, has decreased its reliance on domestic tobacco revenue from 75% to 26% in the same decade. This is all the more remarkable in that in 1965 over 95% of its sales came from nonfiltered cigarettes, Lucky Strike being the big brand.

Of interest, too, are the lines into which they have chosen to diversify. Predictably each has moved into liquor ·and/or food. Philip Morris, for instance, acquired Miller Beer, and L&M acquired J&B Whiskey. Of more interest are the unusual. L&M, for example, acquired Alpo pet foods, and, even further afield, R. J. Reynolds moved into oil, acquiring a crude oil producer operating near Kuwait. Philip Morris appears to have diversified least, partly because of its extraordinarily successful brand Marlboro and, more recently, Merit. In fact, completely against the trend, their tobacco sales moved up from a market share of 12.9% in 1967 to 22% in 1973.

Data on R. J. Reynolds domestic sales versus international sales were not available, nor were those for Ligget & Myers. American Brands is, however, a good example of the problems one runs into in interpreting consolidated data, since in the same period that its domestic sales fell 50%, its international sales rose almost 40%. Philip Morris's apparent relative lack of diversification is due in part to its increase in international sales. Whether one treats overseas sales as part of the "industry" is a thorny nicety.

Little of general interest seems to emerge from these graphs, however. For example, it is clear from Table 5.11 that Philip Morris is in many ways an outlier. This is the one of the four tobacco companies that did not diversify. Instead it concentrated its efforts on the marketing of its best seller, Marlboro. It has since, of course, diversified into Miller Beer. Diversification, however, does not seem to explain the differences in the behavior of rates in the drug industry (Figure 5.1), but there are explanations. Abbott was the major producer of cyclamates and suffered badly when these were banned.

Specific reasons for most irregularities can be found, though these are of no help in building a theory of earnings behavior. One hopes that the idiosyncratic movements do not overwhelm the systematic—otherwise, there is no possibility for theory.

Table 5.8. *Beta Estimates*

			Annual		Monthly	
2111 Cigarettes	24703	American	.508		.607	
	532202	L & M	.568		.498	
	718167	P. Morris	.576		.663	
	461453	Reynolds	.535		.683	
Average:				.551		.613
2335 Drugs	2824	Abbott	.463		.632	
	589331	Merck	.661		.585	
	717081	Pfizer	.676		.843	
	806605	Schering	.606		.662	
Average:				.602		.680
3711 Autos	171196	Chrysler	1.069		1.025	
	345370	Ford	.949		.776	
	370442	General	.854		.655	
Average:				.957		.819
Group I Average:				.680		.693
3241 Cement	370514	Gen. Port.	1.139		1.007	
	451542	Ideal	.805		.912	
	524858	Lehigh	.714		.985	
	542290	Lone Star	.676		.959	
Average:				.834		.948
3310 Steel	87509	Bethlehem	.594		.805	
	760779	Republic	.797		.826	
	912656	U.S.	.653		.793	
Average:				.681		.808
3331 Copper	32393	Anaconda	.842		1.063	
	489314	Kennecott	.148		.693	
	717265	Phelps	.646		.752	
Average:				.545		.836
Group II Average:				.701		.873
1211 Coal	276461	Eastern	1.040		1.053	
	725701	Pittston	.420		1.105	
Average:				.730		1.079
2200 Textiles	206813	Cone	.841		.768	
	235773	Dan River	1.184		.936	
Average:				1.0125		.852
3221 Containers	24843	American	.401		.462	
	33047	Anchor	.847		.839	
	211183	Continental	.525		.649	
	690768	Owen	.570		.586	
Average:				.586		.688
Group III Average:				.729		.827
Grand Mean:				.701		.792

Table 5.9. *Cross-Sectional Correlation Among Beta Residuals*

			Company with Group	Company with Overall Mean
2111 Cigarettes	24703	American	.58	.35
	532202	L & M	.36	.31
	718167	P. Morris	.57	.40
	461753	Reynolds	.56	.30
2335 Drugs	2824	Abbott	.42	.27
	589331	Merck	.50	.25
	717081	Pfizer	.52	.33
	806605	Schering	.44	.23
3711 Autos	171196	Chrysler	.22	.11
	345370	Ford	.33	.23
	370442	General	.42	.33
3241 Cement	370514	Gen. Port	.50	.27
	451542	Ideal	.44	.34
	524858	Lehigh	.46	.18
	542290	Lone Star	.48	.24
3310 Steel	87509	Bethlehem	.56	.47
	760779	Republic	.54	.50
	912656	U.S.	.61	.54
3331 Copper	32393	Anaconda	.51	.34
	489314	Kennecott	.57	.45
	717265	Phelps	.52	.43
1211 Coal	275461	Eastern	.44	.42
	725701	Pittston	.50	.36
2200 Textiles	206813	Cone	.39	.10
	235773	Dan River	.17	− .07
3221 Containers	24843	American	.37	.23
	33047	Anchor	.42	.18
	211183	Continental	.43	.25
	690768	Owen	.38	.20

Table 5.10.   Accounting Return on Equity as Reported

			1936/ 40	1947/ 51	1950/ 60	1958/ 65	1966/ 73	1958/ 73
2111 Cigarettes	24703	American	11.3	12.3	11.7	12.98	13.49	13.23
	532202	L & M	15.0	12.4	10.0	9.61	8.82	9.22
	718167	P. Morris	39.3	12.8	10.2	12.20	17.36	14.48
	461453	Reynolds				19.10	17.90	18.50
Average:			21.1	12.6	11.6			13.93
2335 Drugs	2824	Abbott			14.4	14.20	13.86	14.03
	589331	Merck			14.4	18.13	25.21	21.64
	717081	Pfizer			14.1	15.69	14.96	15.53
	806605	Schering			23.1	18.03	21.88	19.95
Average:					17.9			17.75
3711 Autos	171196	Chrysler	32.3	22.1	10.5	7.54	7.74	4.64
	345370	Ford			14.5	13.14	11.00	12.07
	370442	General	18.1	25.4	21.5	20.19	17.26	18.73
Average:			25.2	23.9	15.5			12.81
Group I Average:					16.4			15.02
3241 Cement	370514	Gen. Port.			20.2	12.16	8.33	12.16
	451542	Ideal			17.8	12.68	9.95	11.31
	524858	Lehigh	4.9	12.0	10.4	5.77	4.50	5.14
	542290	Lone Star	8.3	14.6	14.3	10.43	9.52	9.97
Average:			5.2	14.3	15.7			9.17
3310 Steel	87509	Bethlehem	5.2	12.6	11.8	7.69	7.49	7.59
	760779	Republic	3.9	13.4	12.0	7.71	6.13	6.92
	912656	U.S.	4.0	8.5	10.7	8.00	6.00	7.00
Average:			3.8	11.2	10.8			7.17
3331 Copper	32393	Anaconda	4.4	7.1	7.2	5.19	6.71	5.95
	489314	Kennecott	10.4	15.7	13.8	8.85	11.23	10.04
	717265	Phelps	7.0	19.2	15.3	10.45	13.07	11.76
Average:			8.5	14.6	11.5			9.25
Group II Average:					11.3			8.60
1211 Coal	276461	Eastern				9.18	11.63	10.41
	725701	Pittston				12.84	13.56	13.20
Average:					8.8			11.81
2200 Textiles	206813	Cone			6.3	4.14	5.08	4.61
	235773	Dan River			6.7	7.24	3.83	5.53
Average:					6.9			5.07
3221 Containers	24843	American	10.5	12.3	10.3	9.32	9.94	9.63
	33047	Anchor			13.4	11.70	13.46	12.58
	211183	Continental			9.6	9.15	12.22	10.69
	690768	Owen			13.6	11.39	10.82	11.11
Average:			9.3	10.7	11.6			11.00
Group III Average:					9.9			9.72

Table 5.11. Cigarette Industry Analysis

		Years										
		75	74	73	72	71	70	69	68	67	66	65
Specialization Ratio—Revenue Based (%'s)												
American Brands*	T	65	66	69	71	72	77	80	78	77		
	D	26	28	31	32	35	39	40	59	45		
Ligget & Myers		49	49	51	51	51	55	57	64	68	70	85
Philip Morris^x	D	47	50	50	55	56	61	70				
	T	75	77	79	80	80	85	93				
R. J. Reynolds		69	64	71	73	75	73	76	79	81	84	89
Specialization Ratio—Income Based (%'s)												
American Brands	T	17	20	23	21	17	18	19	12	5		
	D	53	51	52	57	61	67	65	75	83		
Ligget & Myers		41	44	52	38	41	48	47	54	62	69	90
Philip Morris^x	T	91	94	97	97	101	100	94				
	D	68	71	69	68	69	68	69				
R. J. Reynolds		63	50+	83	83	88	86	82	93	86	86	
OP. Inc./Sales—Tobacco Products (%'s)												
American Brands		19	18	18	18	19	18	16	14	14	14	15
Ligget & Myers		13	15	17	12	15	15	14	15	15	9	9
Philip Morris		9	10	12	8	10	10	9	9	9		
R. J. Reynolds		16	19	18	19	22	21	19	19	18	16	
OP. Inc./Sales—Other Products (%'s)												
American Brands		6	7	8	7	7	6	6	8	8		
Ligget & Myers		13	13	11	14	15	14	13	13	11	9	6
Philip Morris			8	8	10	9	11	14				
R. J. Reynolds		21	26	10	11	9	10	13	14	12	13	

*Domestic sales only

+ Due primarily to crude oil subsidiary Aminoil

x All tobacco

Table 5.12.　High-Low Test

Category I

```
                    HIGH-LOW TEST
YEAR          MFAN                     STD      DEV
        LOW     HIGH     DIFF      LOW    HIGH

  1    0.106   0.144    0.038     0.04   0.07
  2    0.114   0.144    0.030     0.04   0.07
  3    0.118   0.143    0.025     0.04   0.07
  4    0.118   0.146    0.028     0.02   0.03
  5    0.120   0.149    0.029     0.02   0.03
  6    0.123   0.151    0.028     0.02   0.03
  7    0.124   0.152    0.029     0.02   0.03
  8    0.128   0.149    0.021     0.02   0.03
  9    0.125   0.150    0.024     0.02   0.03
 10    0.121   0.148    0.026     0.02   0.03
 11    0.122   0.148    0.026     0.02   0.03
 12    0.118   0.150    0.032     0.02   0.03
 13    0.117   0.153    0.035     0.02   0.03
 14    0.125   0.155    0.030     0.02   0.03
 15    0.129   0.153    0.024     0.02   0.03
 16    0.129   0.156    0.027     0.02   0.03
```

Category II

```
                    HIGH-LOW TEST
YEAR          MEAN                     STD      DEV
        LOW     HIGH     DIFF      LOW    HIGH

  1    0.063   0.108    0.045     0.01   0.03
  2    0.065   0.105    0.040     0.02   0.03
  3    0.069   0.099    0.030     0.03   0.03
  4    0.069   0.097    0.027     0.01   0.01
  5    0.073   0.094    0.021     0.01   0.01
  6    0.075   0.093    0.018     0.01   0.01
  7    0.077   0.092    0.016     0.01   0.01
  8    0.072   0.096    0.024     0.01   0.01
  9    0.068   0.098    0.031     0.01   0.01
 10    0.065   0.096    0.031     0.01   0.01
 11    0.070   0.095    0.025     0.01   0.01
 12    0.071   0.092    0.021     0.01   0.01
 13    0.065   0.095    0.031     0.01   0.01
 14    0.066   0.097    0.031     0.01   0.01
 15    0.078   0.102    0.024     0.01   0.01
 16    0.092   0.115    0.024     0.01   0.01
```

Table 5.12.   *Continued*

Category.III

HIGH-LOW TEST

YEAR	MEAN			STD	DEV
	LOW	HIGH	DIFF	LOW	HIGH
1	0.071	0.123	0.053	0.03	0.02
2	0.077	0.118	0.040	0.04	0.03
3	0.079	0.117	0.038	0.04	0.02
4	0.080	0.118	0.038	0.01	0.01
5	0.084	0.116	0.032	0.01	0.01
6	0.086	0.115	0.029	0.01	0.01
7	0.086	0.119	0.032	0.01	0.01
8	0.085	0.119	0.034	0.01	0.01
9	0.081	0.120	0.040	0.01	0.02
10	0.078	0.117	0.039	0.01	0.01
11	0.075	0.117	0.042	0.01	0.02
12	0.075	0.114	0.039	0.01	0.01
13	0.076	0.113	0.037	0.01	0.01
14	0.075	0.108	0.033	0.01	0.01
15	0.078	0.111	0.034	0.01	0.01
16	0.086	0.112	0.026	0.01	0.01

Category II & III

HIGH-LOW TEST

YEAR	MEAN			STD	DEV
	LOW	HIGH	DIFF	LOW	HIGH
1	0.063	0.117	0.054	0.02	0.02
2	0.068	0.113	0.046	0.03	0.03
3	0.070	0.110	0.041	0.03	0.03
4	0.071	0.109	0.038	0.01	0.01
5	0.073	0.108	0.035	0.01	0.01
6	0.076	0.107	0.030	0.01	0.01
7	0.079	0.106	0.027	0.01	0.01
8	0.079	0.106	0.027	0.01	0.01
9	0.074	0.108	0.035	0.01	0.01
10	0.068	0.108	0.040	0.01	0.01
11	0.069	0.108	0.039	0.01	0.01
12	0.070	0.104	0.034	0.01	0.01
13	0.069	0.104	0.035	0.01	0.01
14	0.068	0.104	0.036	0.01	0.01
15	0.078	0.106	0.028	0.01	0.01
16	0.089	0.114	0.025	0.01	0.01

Table 5.12. *Continued*

All 29 Companies

YEAR	HIGH-LOW TEST MEAN			STD DEV	
	LOW	HIGH	DIFF	LOW	HIGH
1	0.071	0.135	0.064	0.03	0.05
2	0.078	0.132	0.054	0.03	0.05
3	0.081	0.129	0.048	0.04	0.05
4	0.083	0.129	0.046	0.01	0.02
5	0.084	0.131	0.047	0.01	0.02
6	0.087	0.130	0.044	0.01	0.02
7	0.089	0.130	0.041	0.01	0.02
8	0.087	0.131	0.044	0.01	0.02
9	0.083	0.133	0.049	0.01	0.02
10	0.078	0.133	0.055	0.01	0.02
11	0.077	0.134	0.057	0.01	0.02
12	0.075	0.134	0.060	0.01	0.02
13	0.073	0.136	0.062	0.01	0.02
14	0.075	0.137	0.062	0.01	0.02
15	0.085	0.135	0.050	0.01	0.02
16	0.097	0.137	0.040	0.01	0.02

Figure 5.1.   Tobacco Industry Rates of Return

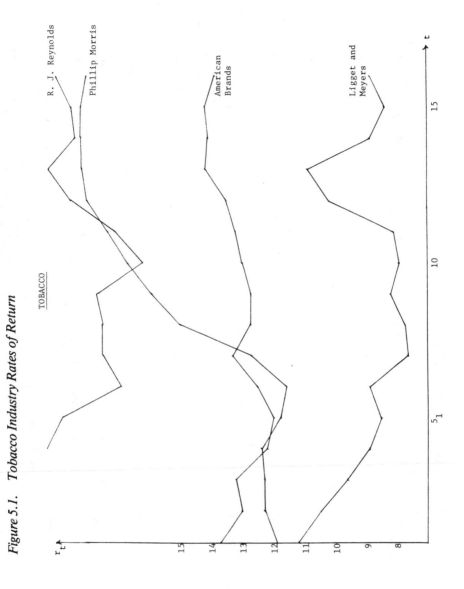

Figure 5.2.   Drug Industry Rates of Return

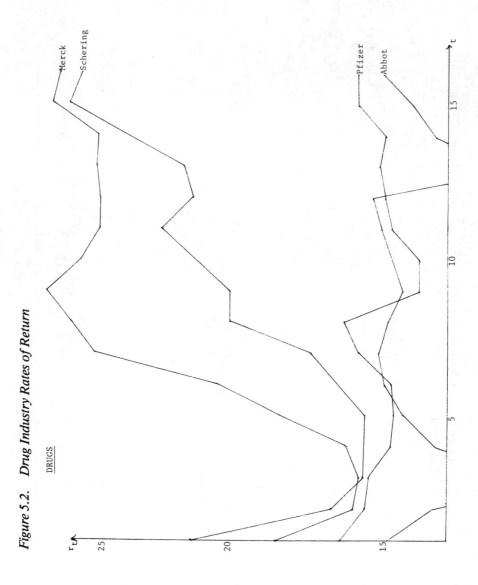

Figure 5.3. Automobile Industry Rates of Return

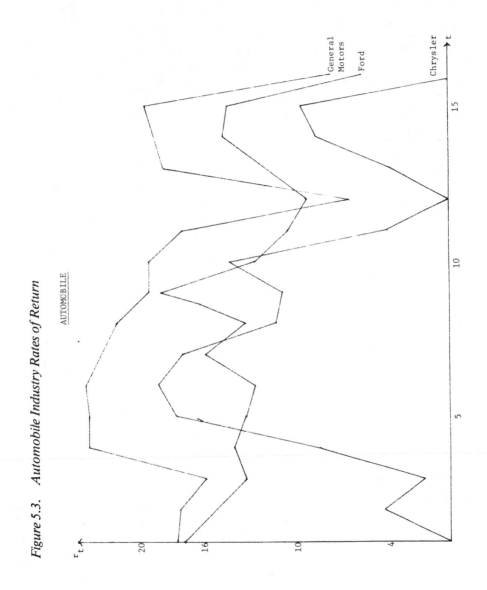

6

Some Econometric Issues

The model proposed for empirical investigation is an endogenous-lagged model with a possibly serially correlated error structure. The combination creates a nontrivial problem of inconsistency while the lag alone generates small sample bias. These two problems are treated in more detail below. The fact that the model is being estimated across a number of companies suggests the possibility of either pooling or using Zellner's method of seemingly unrelated regression. This, too, is discussed below. The empirical investigation involves the estimation of a regression parameter for each company and then a comparison of these parameters across the entire sample. Since the estimator involves statistical error, the possible difficulties this creates and some potential solutions are elaborated on.

Endogenous Lags

The model that was proposed to capture the hypothesized reversion process was of the form:

$$r_t = \alpha + (1 - \lambda\delta)r_{t-1} + \lambda\varrho_t^e - \lambda(1-\delta)\varrho_{t-1}^e + u_t \tag{6.1}$$

This was converted into the following differenced form that was more suitable for regression purposes since a) the original used three variables to estimate only two parameters, and b) because it virtually eliminates the endogenous lag.

$$r_t - r_{t-1} = \alpha + \lambda(\varrho_t^e - \varrho_{t-1}^e) + \lambda\delta(\varrho_{t-1}^e - r_{t-1}) + u_t \tag{6.2}$$

Assume for the moment that we did estimate the equation (6.1) and substitute alternative notation for ease on the eye when we have:

$$Y_t = \theta_0 + \theta_1 Y_{t-1} + \theta_2 X_t + u_t \tag{6.3}$$

where the Y's are endogenous variables and the X's are exogenous. Using small letters to denote deviations from the mean, we can write (6.3) as

$$y_t = \theta_1 y_{t-1} + \theta_2 x_t + \theta_3 x_{t-1} + (u_t - \bar{u}_t) \tag{6.4}$$

Rather than attack this directly, consider first the simpler model

$$y_t = \theta_1 y_{t-1} \tag{6.5}$$

and assume that the error terms are i.i.d. Using OLS to estimate the parameter, one has

$$\hat{\theta}_1 = \frac{\Sigma y_t y_{t-1}}{\Sigma y_{t-1}^2} \tag{6.6}$$

(Summation subscripts will be omitted throughout unless there is a possibility of confusion.) Substituting (6.5) we have

$$\theta_1 = \theta_1 + \frac{\Sigma y_{t-1}(u_t - \bar{u}_t)}{\Sigma y_{t-1}^2} \tag{6.7}$$

Unlike ordinary regression involving an exogenous variable on the right, this last term does not necessarily tend to zero. The reason is that while the u_t term is independent by assumption of y_{t-1}, the $\bar{u}_t$ is not, containing as it does a u_{t-1}. The result is bias even in small samples. The nature of this bias has been explored in depth by Hurwicz (1950), who showed that the bias was on the order of $-2/n$ where n is the number of observations. Given the standard error in our estimates, this implies that with 20 observations there is a bias of 10%, i.e., the true value is roughly 10% higher than the sample estimate.

Turning back to the complete model, it may be demonstrated that the introduction of an exogenous variable decreases this bias. In a Monte Carlo study, Malinvaud (1961) showed that the bias with the exogenous variable included was of the order of 8%. He concludes in his 1970 text:

> In short, these results confirm that the theory developed for regression models is not applicable just as it is to autoregression models. But they suggest that in practice no serious error is committed if we apply the usual methods conceived for regression models to the treatment of the autoregressive models.

Since an exogenous variable and its lagged value are present in (6.1), this suggests that no serious errors will be present if OLS is used to estimate this equation. This conclusion is in no way altered if we estimate equation (6.2) instead, since it is merely a simple rearrangement of (6.1). Ordinary least squares were therefore used in this study.

Autocorrelated Errors

The above, of course, assumes that the error terms are i.i.d. Where this assumption does not hold, the bias can be much greater. Assume by way of example that the error structure of the model is

$$u_t = \varrho u_{t-1} + \varepsilon_t$$

where ε_t is i.i.d. In another Monte Carlo study, Griliches (1961) showed that for low values of θ_1 and high values of ϱ the bias can be as high as 66%. The particularly disturbing feature of this is that it is difficult to estimate the degree of serial correlation in the errors. The Durbin-Watson statistic that applies to models without lagged endogenous variables does not apply (at least in theory) to models with lagged endogenous variables. There are, however, several more comforting features.

First, Durbin (1970) subsequently developed a variation of the Durbin-Watson d statistic, denoted h, which can be used on large samples to detect autocorrelation in the errors in the presence of endogenous variables on the right. Second, Malinvaud (1970) has demonstrated that the existence of an exogenous term in the model reduces the bias considerably. If the variability of the exogenous variable exceeds that of the errors and its coefficient is not near zero, the bias can shrink to almost negligible proportions. To this must be added the conclusions that Kenkel (1974) draws from a Monte Carlo study of a model similar to (6.2). This was essentially that for small samples the upper tail of the Durbin-Watson statistic d outperformed the h statistic in detecting autocorrelation and does it quite successfully.

Since in this study the Durbin-Watson d values were by and large above the critical value in the upper tail, indicating that serial correlation was probably low if it entered at all, the decision was made to use OLS throughout.

Zellner's Method

It was demonstrated earlier that the CAPM did not account for all interfirm effects, i.e., a cross-sectional correlation of the errors revealed a fair amount of positive interdependence. This obviously carries over to model (6.2), which was estimated across a number of firms. This suggests that the use of Zellner's method might be appropriate. In vector notation we have for each equation

$$y_i = X_i\beta_i + u_i \quad i = 1, 2, \ldots, n \tag{6.8}$$

One combines these equations in a diagonal matrix of the form

$$
\begin{bmatrix} y_1 \\ \cdot \\ \cdot \\ \cdot \\ y_n \end{bmatrix} = \begin{bmatrix} X_1 & 0 & \cdots & 0 \\ 0 & X_2 & \cdots & 0 \\ \cdot & & & \cdot \\ \cdot & & & \cdot \\ 0 & 0 & & X_n \end{bmatrix} \times \begin{bmatrix} \beta_1 \\ \beta_2 \\ \cdot \\ \cdot \\ \beta_n \end{bmatrix} + \begin{bmatrix} u_1 \\ u_2 \\ \cdot \\ \cdot \\ u_n \end{bmatrix} \tag{6.9}
$$

The n equations are then estimated simultaneously.

The problem with the method is that the errors are heteroscedastic. Zellner suggests running the regressions independently first and using the results to compute the Aitken matrix. The first stage of this two-state procedure clearly induces estimation error, and the size of this error must be balanced against the gain in efficiency that the second stage generates. Since the method reduces to OLS when the x_i are identical, it is obvious that this gain is greater when the correlation between the x_i's is small. Similarly, the essence of the method is the cross-correlation in the error terms, which must be high to make the method worthwhile. While the latter condition is reasonably met, the former, unfortunately, is not. The exogenous variable used was the market rate effectively, which was the same for all firms. As a result, the expected gain is small. The decision was therefore made to concentrate on independent OLS.

Estimation Errors

The coefficient λ was estimated for each company and the results were regressed on various explanatory variables. Following Hanushek (1974) we can formally set the model up as

$$
Y_i = \beta_i Z_i + w_i \tag{6.10}
$$

where the β_i coefficients of interest to be estimated and

$$
\beta = X_y + v \tag{6.11}
$$

where y are the coefficients of interest in explaining the various β_i. We do not, however, know the true values of β_i. We have instead

$$
\hat{\beta} = \beta + u \tag{6.12}
$$

which leads to the equation

$$\hat{\beta} = X_y + (u + v) = X_y + E \tag{6.13}$$

The presence of the u term induces heteroscedasticity. Ideally one should use generalized least squares to estimate this last equation using information derived from the estimation of β_i.

Little or nothing is known, however, about the small sample properties of this procedure. Furthermore, heteroscedasticity induces problems of inefficiency rather than of bias. Given this it was felt that the considerable extra programming effort was not merited at this point. It remains an area for investigation at a later stage.

An alternative method to escape the above problem is to aggregate the estimated coefficients. A similar procedure has been used with success in the finance literature. For the purposes of doing cross-sectional analyses of the systematic risk coefficient beta in the CAPM, portfolios are created. Typically some 500 or more betas are estimated and some 10 or 20 portfolios created. These aggregated betas are then used in the subsequent analysis.

The procedure is clearly applicable. For its successful application, it requires a large number of estimating equations and the assumption that the portfolios so formed are in some sense homogeneous. At this stage of our analysis of accounting numbers the latter assumption is difficult to justify. In fact, the basic question being addressed here is whether one can even begin to talk in terms of homogeneous portfolios at all when it comes to accounting numbers or whether firms are so idiosyncratic that any aggregation is misleading. Further, one has the problem of providing sufficient data. For instance, it was possible in this study to come up with only 29 firms that could be classified on a barrier-to-entry basis. The method was therefore discarded for this study, though it clearly needs to be pursued in further studies.

7

Empirical Results

We are finally in a position to draw everything together and measure the theory developed thus far against the data. The data used, as mentioned earlier, consist of 29 companies drawn from Bain's 1956 study and Mann's 1966 study on barriers to entry. This chapter discusses in turn the results of tests of the null hypothesis, the alternative hypothesis, and the joint hypothesis. It concludes with a discussion of the predictive power of the model.

The Maintained Hypothesis

The accounting rate and the market rate as defined earlier were combined in one file and differenced according to the model (5.4). Regressions were then run for each company and the results tabulated. These may be found in Tables 7.1 through 7.6. The routine used for this purpose was the IMSL subroutine RLSEP, which is available in both single and double precision and appears to be highly efficient.

The first six columns of the table are self-explanatory. The model as presented and tested above conformed (at least in theory) with the *a priori* theoretical considerations. Given that one of the goals of this study is to arrive at a superior model for the prediction of earnings, there is clearly a case for examining alternative specifications, which while not so strongly driven by *a priori* theory, might lead to still better predictions. One hopes, too, that these alternatives will lead to deeper insights into the process generating earnings. Five alternative models were used.

1) Naive: $X_t = X_{t-1} + u_t$

2) Mean: $X_t = \dfrac{1}{n} \sum\limits_{j=1}^{n} X_{t-j} + u_t$

3) Time: $X_t = a + bt + u_t$

4) Auto: $X_t = c + dX_{t-1} + u_t$

5) Model: $X_t = (1 - \lambda\delta)X_{t-1} + \lambda X_t^e - \lambda(1-\delta)X_{t-1}^e + u_t$

The mean absolute deviation and mean square error over the 29 companies are
reported at the base of the tables. Since the autoregressive model is the closest
competitor to the model used by this study, their individual errors are reported
along with those of the model.

Tables 7.1 through 7.3 are based upon the use of the individual security
rates as a surrogate for the term ϱ_t^e in (5.4). The precise formulation used in
each case was

1) $\varrho_t^e = \mu - \theta(\varrho_{t-1} - \varrho_{t-1}^e)$

2) $\varrho_t^e = \varrho_{t-1}^e + \theta(\varrho_{t-1} - \varrho_{t-1}^e)$

3) $\varrho_t^e = \varrho_{t-1}^e + \beta\theta(\varrho_{t-1} - \varrho_{t-1})$

Arguments for each of these were given in Chapters 4 and 5.

It is readily apparent that the first model is an almost complete failure. In
the other two cases, the signs of the adjustment coefficients are as predicted
with only a very few exceptions. The adjustment model in this sense is fairly
robust. The lambdas are positive and the deltas are, with few exceptions,
negative. This corresponds with the theoretical specifications. The values of
lambda are small, but roughly what one would expect. The average book life
was on the order of 20 years, implying that roughly that many years would
have to pass before the book had been replaced. This, in turn, suggests an
adjustment parameter on the order of 0.05, which is the error of magnitude
shown by most firms.

The values of delta are larger than the simple model would predict. (This
was discussed in Chapter 5, where reasons for this were adduced.) In brief, the
model as it stands assumes that the input vector is locally constant. Obviously it
is not. Inflation is only one factor that destroys this assumption. Varying
capacity utilization is another. Changes in wage rates and raw materials are yet
other factors that are likely to affect the model and make the assumption of
local constancy nonviable. These factors will directly affect the value of delta,
as demonstrated in Chapter 5, and indirectly the value of lambda. The degree
of bias is not known at present. Clearly this will have to be pursued in later
research.

It should be borne in mind that this study is intended as only the first of a
number of studies that will feed off one another. To build the adaptive expectations model, it was necessary to understand the behavior of earnings, which
was unknown. But to gain understanding of the unknown behavior of
earnings, it was necessary to assume a first-pass adaptive-expectations model.
With the insights gained into the behavior of earnings, more appropriate
adaptive-expectations models can be built leading to yet more refined earnings

models, and so on. This is closely related to the need to initially regress on one company over a fairly long time period in which the generating mechanism is highly likely to be nonstationary. With the insights gained, one hopes to be able to pool and thereby shorten the time period needed and so arrive at more refined models again. The process promises to take years since it clearly involves a highly complex subject. This book claims to have broken new ground. It does not claim to have answered all the questions. There is much left for future research.

The explanatory power of the model may be gauged by the reported R-squared's. Each regression was run over 15 observations and used three explanatory variables, including the constant. The degrees of freedom are therefore $(2,12)$ and the associated $F(0.05) = 3.89$. From the relationship

$$R^2 = \{1 + \frac{n-k}{(k-1)F}\}^{-1}$$

$$= \{1 + \frac{15-3}{2 \times 3.74}\}^{-1}$$

$$= 38.4\%$$

we have the associated critical values for R-squared. These are exceeded in Table 7.1 only by 3, in Table 7.2 only by 7, and in Table 7.3 only by 11. These are disappointingly low. They may, however, be compared with the widely accepted general model for accounting earnings, the random walk or martingale, which would predict no explanation at all.

The predictive power of each of these models was tested with the results below. Two sets of predictions were tested—a one-period-ahead extrapolation and a random interpolation. In each case the model posited was compared with the simple autoregressive model on a mean square error basis. The tests performed were a paired t-test and a Wilcoxon test for matched samples. Details of these tests are reported in Chapter 4. First, we report the extrapolation results.

	Paired Sample t-Test	Wilcoxon Z Value
Table 7.1	0.70	1.31
Table 7.2	1.92	1.74
Table 7.3	1.80	1.61

A t-value of 1.7 is significant at the 5% level as is a z-value of 1.65. It is apparent that two of the three t-values are significant at this level, as is one of the z-values, with the second one marginally significant at this level. These results must be tempered by the fact that there is cross-sectional correlation among the equations, however. This will reduce the variance estimate and make these results look better than they really are. The degree of statistical bias is, however, difficult to estimate.

The interpolation results were spotty. As discussed earlier, random numbers were generated and the mean square error of predicting that particular year was calculated. The major problem here is that a large number of runs are required to arrive at statistically meaningful results. A limited computer budget precluded this. However, the runs that were done all revealed interpolation results that were no better than those reported above. In other words, results were worse on average. For example, one output of the exponentially smoothed model was as follows:

	Naive	Mean	Time	Auto	Model
MAD	0.01457	0.01879	0.01575	0.01528	0.01350
MSE	0.00053	0.00071	0.00049	0.00051	0.00037

What is potentially interesting here is that all of the models tended to converge. This suggests that over the long run earnings might be growing fairly steadily, enabling a simple time-based model to be a reasonable predictor. On the other hand, in the short run an autoregressive model or the model posited here might be superior. Since the interpolation results are in general worse, I will not comment on them further.

The model was then run using $\alpha + \beta Rm$ as a surrogate for ϱ—this follows the CAPM and was discussed earlier. The results of this were disappointing so the model was run with the assumption of a β of one. The specific models run were:

1) $\varrho_t^e = \mu - \theta(Rm_{t-1} - \varrho_{t-1}^e)$

2) $\varrho_t^e = \varrho_{t-1}^e + \theta(Rm_{t-1} + \varrho_{t-1}^e)$

3) $\varrho_t^e = Rm_{t-1}$

These are reported on in Tables 7.4 through 7.6.

As before the R-squareds are low—in fact lower than in the first tables. Moreover, the lambdas are not all positive. However, as we shall see in the next section, the lambdas are a function of asset life. Also, the use of the actual value of Rm turns out to create a predictive model that is significantly better than its nearest competitor. Given that the use of Rm is cheap, in that one does not have to look for the security return, this might prove to be a useful model in sharpening our predictive results of earnings. The actual results are shown below.

	Paired Sample t-Test	Wilcoxon Z Value
Table 7.4	0.90	0.77
Table 7.5	1.18	1.39
Table 7.6	2.04	1.65

Of these, only the last are significant at the 5% level. That they are, however, seems to indicate that the market as a whole tends to rise in the year that earnings rise and in that sense to lead earnings and, therefore, to be of use in predicting earnings.

The Null Hypothesis

Having established that the model is a reasonably valid representation of the adjustment process that is at work, it is possible to test the null hypothesis that the adjustment parameter varies according to barriers to entry. A one-way analysis of variance on the λ's in 7.3 was performed across the three groups and yielded an F value of 2.686, which is significant at the 8.5 percent level. Since the problem is really to explain why Group I's mean rate of profit is so much higher than the other two groups, a second analysis of variance was run across these two categories. Rather surprisingly the significance fell—the test yielded an F value of 1.999, which is significant at the 16.6% level only. The conclusion is that by classical testing procedures we must reject the null hypothesis that the rate of reversion is a function of the barriers to entry.

The test was repeated by running a dummy variable regression of lambdas on barriers to entry. As discussed earlier, the coefficients of this regression should be positive. Almost without exception they were negative, indicating that, if anything, lambdas are positively correlated with barriers to entry and not negatively correlated as predicted. This was further confirmed by running a Jonkheere's test, which tests for differences both in lambdas and direction. The results from two of these are −0.47 and −0.93. All the others were in the same region. In other words, there is no indication that the lambdas vary across barriers to entry, and if they do, it is in the wrong direction.

In fairness to Bain and Mann, two things must be said. The testing procedure is sufficiently crude, as are the operationalizations that 8.5% could be considered a remarkable result. Only further work will confirm this rejection. It must also be emphasized that the companies they studied have changed dramatically in the past two decades. As already pointed out, R. J. Reynolds is today a large crude oil producer, and at the time of writing, Kennecott was still a large coal producer. It is quite probable that Bain today would feel that testing his theory on the companies as they are presently constituted amounts almost to knocking a straw man. Be that as it may, it remains true that the Group I companies, however altered, are still showing an extremely high return relative to the others in the sample. If the Bain hypothesis no longer applies because of diversification, there is no longer any explanation at all for these huge cross-sectional differences. Moreover, it is then unclear whether the null hypothesis applies to the earlier period either.

The Alternative Hypothesis

The adjustment parameters were then regressed against the average book life of the firms. In other words a cross-sectional regression containing 29 observations was performed on the lambdas, which had been derived from the longitudinal regressions on the model. This was done for two averages. The first book life average was calculated over all 16 years in the study. The second average was calculated over the last four years only. The reason for this latter was obvious. The idea was simply that the more recent years would have more influence on the adjustment parameter than the earlier years. As it turns out there is nothing in it and the results of the 16-year average may be found below.

	Coefficient	R^2	F	R^2	F
Table 7.1	−0.014	2%	—	8%	1.21
Table 7.2	−0.002	10%	3.07	14%	2.20
Table 7.3	−0.002	20%	6.78	17%	2.69
Table 7.4	−0.005	7%	2.16	7%	1.08
Table 7.5	−0.004	23%	8.06	17%	2.74
Table 7.6	−0.003	28%	10.50	17%	2.75

The first three columns report the coefficient, R-squared, and associated F value for each regression of lambda on life. It is noteworthy that in each case the coefficient is negative as predicted. This suggests that despite the overall weakness of the results, there is something here that might repay future research. It might be noted again here that in a small subsidiary piece of research where lambda was regressed on growth as well as life, considerably larger explanations were achieved. This should not be taken as "proof" of any sort of the model, but it serves as a small indication that as the model is sharpened, it is conceivable that much better results might be obtained.

The second two columns of results are those obtained from regressing lambda on the dummy variables derived from the barriers to entry and discussed above. These are lower than those of the regressions obtained from the life regression, but clearly move with the life regression and therefore suggest that the two explanations might be collinear.

Returning to the regression on life, the critical F value at the 5% level is 4.21. With three out of the six regressions significant, there is a small indication that there might be a significant relationship between life and lambda.

Again, a warning must be entered. In terms of modern decision theory the above results merely constitute information which may or may not enable one to revise one's priors on the topic. They can hardly be construed as conclusive at this state—too many factors have still to be evaluated and specifications improved. The results are, however, suggestive and augur well for further research in this area.

The Joint Hypothesis

The last major question that was left was to test to what extent the two hypotheses were collinear. To this end the residuals from the above equation were calculated and inserted into a one-way analysis of variance identical to that used in testing the null hypothesis. The result showed that barriers to entry explained virtually nothing of the residuals—F values were of the order of 0.15.

The book life was also regressed against the barriers to entry and revealed a highly significant R-squared of 58%. As a further test of collinearity, lambda was regressed on both barriers to entry and life. The results were as follows:

	R^2	F
Table 7.1	8.7%	0.80
Table 7.2	14.7%	1.43
Table 7.3	24.1%	2.64
Table 7.4	10.5%	0.98
Table 7.5	25.4%	2.83
Table 7.6	29.2%	3.43

It is clear that very little extra explanation is gained by combining the two variables.

Obviously the two hypotheses are collinear. This is an interesting result. It suggests that a supposedly economic result *might* be an accounting phenomenon in reality. On the other hand, it might also be true that book life, as calculated here, is highly correlated with economic life, that barriers to entry are a function of capital intensity, and that the accounting explanation is in reality an economic one. As with all collinear phenomena, to break the dilemma it is necessary to gather further data, in this case to find firms whose barriers to entry differ but are not a function of capital intensity. This will have to await further research. Asset lives seem to provide slightly higher explanation, but the two hypotheses are too collinear to separate.

Prediction

With the testing of the model and the related hypotheses complete, we can turn our attention to the predictive ability of the model and to alternative specifications. In the course of testing the model, some alternatives were tried in an attempt to gain insight into the factors driving the model.

First, the accounting rate used above was based on end-of-year book value. A commonly used alternative is the start-of-year book value. This was tried in calculating the rate of accounting profit. Throughout all specifications it yielded consistently inferior predictions for all five models. Just why this should be so is not clear, unless management and the market use the contemporaneous version, which makes it that much more predictable. To give an indication of the difference, the naive model shows a mean square error of 0.805 for the lagged but 0.415 for the contemporaneous version.

A number of alternatives were experimented with for the market rate. The problem that one faces here is that in the usual adjustment one regresses a variable on its own lagged values. This ensures that the dependent and independent variables are of the same magnitude. This is clearly not the case here, since the equity market shows fluctuations that are wildly larger than the accounting rate. Not only that, but different securities show different degrees of volatility. The result is to introduce a great deal of noise into the system for estimating purposes. This was overcome in this study by normalizing the fluctuations in the individual securities by their betas or volatility factors. This procedure is clearly open to debate and one has to admit that no good answer exists at present.

One alternative is to use a single common factor, such as the rate of interest on company bonds. This was done and provides good explanation, but is not a good predictor. Using the contemporaneous rate one has an MSE of 0.00417 for the model and 0.00389 for the autoregressive model. Not all variations of interest rates were tried, and it is true that in this period, the sudden bouts of inflation caused interest rates to move in a different direction to the market so that it is possible that this strategy might, for a different period and for a different grade of bond, give more satisfactory results, but this researcher must report a negative outcome.

As reported above, although the model specified the security specific rate, the actual overall market rate was also used. The idea behind this was to see whether it was the rise and fall in the market as a whole that was driving the results. This appeared to be the case since in Table 7.6 we find an MSE of 0.00297 for the model against an MSE of 0.00389 for the autoregressive model.

This is a cheap, quick, and easy model to use, and I tested it on another entirely random set of data. It yielded similar results. Random numbers were generated and 29 firms were drawn off COMPUSTAT accordingly. The MSE of the model was 0.1300 against 0.1340 for the autoregressive model—not significant, but an improvement. Interestingly, the coefficient of the cross-sectional regression against the lambdas here was a significant -0.003 with an R-squared of 25%. This suggests that the model might have application beyond the firms from Bain's sample. The results from this regression may be found in Table 7.7.

This model was again run on two larger samples. Two sets of 150 companies each were drawn from COMPUSTAT, giving a total of 300 companies. The results can only be described as extremely disappointing. For the large sample the proposed model was clearly outperformed by a simple naive model. The actual results were:

	Naive	Mean	Time	Auto	Model
MAD	0.03622	0.04416	0.04770	0.03932	0.04119
MSE	0.00287	0.00334	0.00384	0.00281	0.00360
MAD	0.04240	0.05847	0.05537	0.04502	0.04811
MSE	0.00509	0.00739	0.00710	0.00527	0.00612

The differences are not statistically significant; however, the estimates clearly indicate that the naive and the autoregressive model are superior.

Why this should be so is unclear given that the model seemed to perform quite well on Bain's data and that since the actual market rate was used, there was no "fitting" of the model specifically to Bain's sample. The only grain of comfort in this is that the regression of lambdas on book life shows a continuing negative correlation as predicted, although the explanation is very low and not significant statistically.

Conclusion

The theoretical model remains intuitively appealing to this researcher at least. Unfortunately, its operationalization and implementation have not proved easy. First, it is extremely difficult to arrive at a well-justified expectation of the equilibrium rate. A number of alternatives were tried with varying success. An exponentially smoothed security rate yields reversion parameters of the right size and sign. The explanation is, however, very low, suggesting that other explanatory variables are missing. This impression is buttressed by the misspecification of many of the delta parameters.

Accepting for the moment the model as reasonably well specified, a test of the null hypothesis revealed that Bain's hypothesis is marginally unacceptable. A test of the alternative hypothesis reveals that it is just possible that the adjustment parameters might be a function of book life. This result holds up over a wide variety of specifications, but in each case is fairly weak. Clearly further work is required before it can be claimed as a definitive result. For example, factors such as growth need to be included in the regression of lambda on book life. Preliminary results indicate that this might strengthen the conclusion.

The clearest result to emerge is that the two hypotheses are highly collinear. This is a new result as far as I am aware and seems to have been established beyond any reasonable doubt. However, this, too, requires further research. It should be possible to track down the book lives of all the companies in Bain's sample, not just the 29 used here. If so this could be an entirely new, albeit minor, addition to our knowledge.

The predictive power of the model turns out to be disappointingly low. However, an examination of the tables reveals that in certain cases the model explains a very high proportion of the variance remaining after the naive model—recall that the model predicts first differences. This being the case, it is possible that the model is appropriate to a certain class of companies and that other explanatory variables are required for others. Classifying firms might possibly lead to yet further insight into the process generating earnings. However, that too will have to await further research.

Table 7.1.

SUMMARY

	CONST.	LAMDA	DELTA	RSQ	DURB	AUTO	MODEL
276461	0.01313	0.04966	-0.94223	15.20	2.38	0.09290	0.08889
725701	0.00563	-0.00067	52.47417	8.79	2.13	0.22546	0.23612
24703	0.00405	0.00984	-2.18511	12.14	2.16	-0.00097	-0.00541
532202	-0.00025	0.01593	-1.11455	3.17	1.51	0.00382	0.00441
718167	0.00379	0.00119	1.13164	0.27	1.07	-0.00605	-0.00727
761753	0.00340	0.01885	-1.01092	10.76	1.91	0.00820	0.00648
206813	0.00009	-0.06801	-0.19485	34.49	1.69	0.03753	0.04240
235773	-0.00043	-0.05845	0.38966	31.61	1.64	-0.01988	-0.00885
2824	0.00087	0.00515	-2.35476	0.32	2.61	0.01283	0.01085
589331	-0.01413	-0.07785	-0.77281	14.96	0.89	-0.00190	-0.00175
717081	-0.00047	0.01019	-0.07297	8.15	1.94	0.00499	0.00028
806605	-0.01894	-0.05481	-1.31552	39.97	1.40	0.00504	-0.02017
24843	0.00728	0.06493	-1.07018	12.32	1.49	0.04233	0.03543
33047	-0.00613	-0.02949	-0.57581	4.57	2.10	-0.02327	-0.00744
211183	0.00638	0.03311	-0.96209	4.66	1.82	0.02290	0.01157
690768	0.00310	0.02304	-1.04920	1.43	2.54	-0.00043	-0.00003
370514	-0.00668	-0.00838	-1.08300	0.93	1.22	-0.05349	-0.05023
451542	0.00246	0.02881	-1.10409	1.30	1.72	0.02613	0.01825
524858	0.00183	-0.02312	1.64443	18.71	1.34	-0.01457	-0.03306
542290	-0.00306	-0.02384	-0.82656	4.71	1.75	-0.01182	-0.01692
87509	-0.00052	-0.00876	-1.88813	0.60	2.48	0.06024	0.04310
760779	0.00070	0.02876	-1.09767	1.48	1.46	0.06478	0.06267
912656	-0.00303	-0.04835	-1.20220	3.08	1.88	0.06882	0.05100
32393	-0.00139	-0.10333	-0.06253	30.55	2.75	0.02037	0.00593
489314	-0.00058	-0.13387	-0.09261	16.71	2.14	0.00988	-0.06142
717265	-0.01531	-0.12696	-0.85336	9.99	2.35	0.00011	-0.01886
171196	0.03093	-0.06907	1.62118	58.80	1.07	-0.11573	-0.09169
345370	0.03697	0.00627	-28.69902	43.82	2.54	-0.06622	-0.07428
370442	-0.00464	-0.20578	-0.09045	30.47	2.74	-0.11630	-0.08028

	NAIVE	MEAN	TIME	AUTO	MODEL
MAD	0.03959	0.04471	0.04329	0.03921	0.03776
MSE	0.00415	0.00400	0.00403	0.00389	0.00361

The Prediction of Corporate Earnings

Table 7.2.

SUMMARY

	CONST.	LAMDA	DELTA	RSQ	DURB	AUTO	MODEL
276461	0.00456	0.02038	0.55011	14.38	2.45	0.09290	0.09228
725701	-0.00225	0.08715	-0.92647	38.94	2.37	0.22546	0.22263
24703	0.00112	0.01902	-0.05210	31.49	2.43	-0.00097	-0.00599
532202	-0.00162	0.03249	-0.43652	33.37	2.21	0.00382	0.00771
718167	0.00481	0.00794	0.46977	7.02	1.37	-0.00605	-0.00533
761753	0.00029	0.02708	-0.40760	27.20	1.90	0.00820	0.00328
206813	-0.00546	0.04070	-1.87711	31.92	1.83	0.03753	0.04665
235773	-0.00344	0.07037	-1.34061	30.05	1.11	-0.01988	0.00876
2824	0.00057	0.05653	-0.95193	13.75	2.62	0.01283	0.01904
589331	0.00873	0.09642	-1.12330	40.53	1.89	-0.00190	0.02309
717081	0.00019	0.02241	-0.46296	27.07	2.13	0.00499	0.00445
806605	0.00150	0.06925	-0.27309	35.52	1.21	0.00504	0.01058
24843	0.00555	0.08576	-0.72393	47.28	1.44	0.04233	0.03155
33047	0.00197	0.08037	-0.96192	64.45	2.39	-0.02327	-0.00447
211183	0.00478	0.05158	-0.41497	35.66	2.05	0.02290	0.00361
690768	0.00368	0.03982	-0.75700	4.42	2.38	-0.00043	0.00092
370514	-0.00311	0.03786	-0.78843	45.71	1.30	-0.05349	-0.03616
451542	0.00742	0.09985	-0.99931	32.62	2.14	0.02613	0.03708
524858	0.00312	0.05193	-1.55650	29.12	1.77	-0.01457	-0.02344
542290	0.00149	0.01971	-1.81404	16.72	1.82	-0.01182	-0.00963
87509	0.00416	0.09465	-0.99491	30.04	3.01	0.06024	0.05451
760779	0.00772	0.12484	-0.97860	40.55	1.73	0.06478	0.05517
912656	0.00434	0.08483	-0.99149	22.00	2.80	0.06882	0.05124
32393	-0.00196	0.06855	-1.61807	33.84	2.53	0.02037	0.02837
489314	0.00442	0.08837	-1.74114	37.95	2.36	0.00988	-0.03948
717265	0.00350	0.11741	-1.48608	32.56	2.34	0.00011	0.01760
171196	-0.00134	0.09801	-0.94930	40.59	2.04	-0.11573	-0.06628
345370	-0.00884	0.07280	-2.61659	42.59	2.36	-0.06622	-0.01500
370442	0.01312	0.05998	-3.64482	35.91	2.48	-0.11630	-0.04180

	NAIVE	MEAN	TIME	AUTO	MODEL
MAD	0.03959	0.04471	0.04329	0.03921	0.03331
MSE	0.00415	0.00400	0.00403	0.00389	0.00288

Table 7.3.

SUMMARY

	CONST.	LAMDA	DELTA	RSQ	DURB	AUTO	MODEL
276461	0.00254	0.01085	0.01619	14.65	2.52	0.09290	0.09671
725701	-0.00332	0.05173	-1.17489	44.88	2.61	0.22546	0.21601
24703	0.00377	0.03521	-0.95038	25.26	1.99	-0.00097	-0.00325
532202	0.00557	0.09043	-1.20952	39.41	2.27	0.00382	0.01049
718167	0.00475	0.01327	-1.05311	2.02	1.19	-0.00605	-0.00389
761753	0.00487	0.04753	-0.82909	30.04	1.86	0.00820	0.00376
206813	-0.00164	0.03132	-2.86567	45.94	1.92	0.03753	0.04951
235773	-0.00343	0.04209	-2.04244	45.53	1.15	-0.01988	0.01637
2824	0.00208	0.04418	-1.56004	14.52	2.60	0.01283	0.02193
589331	0.01915	0.07126	-1.78431	32.79	1.14	-0.00190	0.02094
717081	0.00045	0.02458	-0.96743	14.54	1.84	0.00499	0.00656
806605	0.00425	0.06329	-1.10769	21.30	0.79	0.00504	0.01488
24843	0.01508	0.14431	-1.22478	50.49	1.43	0.04233	0.03298
33047	0.00089	0.05111	-1.38824	65.44	1.87	-0.02327	-0.00391
211183	0.00609	0.05732	-1.15573	27.37	1.51	0.02290	0.01007
690768	0.00327	0.02491	-1.05544	4.10	2.40	-0.00043	0.00033
370514	-0.00412	0.02117	-1.24340	37.94	0.97	-0.05349	-0.03661
451542	0.00378	0.05198	-1.23005	28.07	1.94	0.02613	0.03678
524858	0.00295	0.03811	-1.96252	38.48	1.62	-0.01457	-0.02250
542290	0.00123	0.00839	-3.81373	25.45	1.48	-0.01182	-0.00955
87509	0.00029	0.02644	-1.25634	21.10	2.86	0.06024	0.05442
760779	0.00188	0.04090	-1.13451	30.86	1.74	0.06478	0.05837
912656	-0.00028	0.02157	-1.25105	10.18	2.45	0.06882	0.05616
32393	-0.00300	0.01991	-2.50518	38.71	2.73	0.02037	0.02052
489314	0.00068	0.03072	-2.60452	37.76	2.42	0.00988	-0.06022
717265	-0.00095	0.02602	-2.40246	22.99	2.38	0.00011	0.00087
171196	0.00063	0.07153	-1.82323	53.62	1.64	-0.11573	-0.04721
345370	0.00690	0.09006	-2.66415	50.18	2.57	-0.06622	-0.00375
370442	0.03153	0.04388	-5.92657	48.89	2.72	-0.11630	-0.04085

	NAIVE	MEAN	TIME	AUTO	MODEL
MAD	0.03959	0.04471	0.04329	0.03921	0.03308
MSE	0.00415	0.00400	0.00403	0.00389	0.00283

The Prediction of Corporate Earnings

Table 7.4.

SUMMARY

	CONST.	LAMDA	DELTA	RSQ	DURB	AUTO	MODEL
276461	0.01560	0.13043	-0.63125	19.19	2.56	0.09290	0.07363
725701	0.02246	0.18276	-0.68014	21.31	1.99	0.22546	0.20988
24703	0.00234	0.01346	-0.76008	2.86	2.18	-0.00097	-0.00650
532202	0.00057	0.04418	-0.35988	20.55	1.88	0.00382	-0.00085
718167	0.00063	-0.00778	-2.56540	13.38	1.11	-0.00605	-0.00640
761753	0.01006	0.06436	-0.71212	24.61	1.59	0.00820	-0.00172
206813	0.00625	0.01819	-2.68022	13.37	1.57	0.03753	0.02776
235773	0.00442	-0.01103	5.43034	18.26	1.30	-0.01988	-0.02033
2824	-0.01242	-0.06834	-0.87671	5.15	2.75	0.01283	0.02249
599331	0.00202	-0.01377	-0.77647	0.41	0.88	-0.00190	-0.00406
717081	-0.00883	-0.02963	-1.36746	18.43	1.75	0.00499	0.00514
806605	-0.03336	-0.10835	-1.34399	42.50	1.27	0.00504	-0.00176
24843	-0.00104	0.00119	7.00278	1.38	1.78	0.04233	0.04000
33047	-0.03133	-0.23290	-0.68431	70.76	1.57	-0.02327	0.02560
211183	-0.00618	-0.04764	-1.11465	11.38	2.05	0.02290	0.02296
690768	0.00345	0.01888	-0.89576	0.66	2.56	-0.00043	-0.00013
370514	-0.00751	-0.01109	-1.25575	0.56	1.22	-0.05349	-0.05033
451542	0.01964	0.15034	-0.86403	31.92	1.61	0.02613	-0.00387
524858	0.00071	-0.06838	0.09366	27.19	1.33	-0.01457	-0.02227
542290	-0.00515	-0.04046	-0.77002	8.96	1.99	-0.01182	-0.01373
87509	-0.00220	-0.03354	-0.53055	2.29	2.35	0.06024	0.05021
760779	-0.00344	-0.04335	-0.49795	2.59	1.45	0.06478	0.06768
912656	-0.00604	-0.05009	-0.76041	3.48	1.87	0.06882	0.06710
32393	-0.00578	-0.15196	-0.32530	22.23	2.17	0.02037	0.04164
489314	-0.01736	-0.19781	-0.67156	14.29	2.00	0.00988	0.02099
717265	-0.01486	-0.14455	-0.71603	13.09	2.05	0.00011	0.01132
171196	0.02578	0.09257	-1.67867	26.30	1.78	-0.11573	-0.13200
345370	0.01478	-0.17295	0.56475	64.06	2.51	-0.06622	-0.05353
370442	0.02778	-0.01237	9.75285	25.63	2.65	-0.11630	-0.11466

	NAIVE	MEAN	TIME	AUTO	MODEL
MAD	0.03959	0.04471	0.04329	0.03921	0.03857
MSE	0.00415	0.00400	0.00403	0.00389	0.00361

Table 7.5.

SUMMARY

	CONST.	LAMDA	DELTA	RSQ	DURB	AUTO	MODEL
276461	0.00341	0.00599	1.36936	0.96	2.43	0.09290	0.09288
725701	-0.00216	-0.02002	0.08366	2.00	2.22	0.22546	0.24257
24703	0.00134	0.01798	-0.46940	19.55	1.90	-0.00097	-0.00158
532202	-0.00065	-0.00676	-3.65213	9.34	1.61	0.00382	-0.00084
718167	0.00445	0.00753	-0.31728	2.32	1.24	-0.00605	-0.00556
761753	-0.00158	-0.01087	-0.77065	2.20	2.15	0.00820	0.00596
206813	0.00532	-0.06754	-0.77985	17.98	1.51	0.03753	0.01018
235773	-0.00048	-0.03941	-0.32121	4.45	1.34	-0.01988	-0.02979
2824	-0.00235	-0.00928	0.93990	1.62	2.55	0.01283	0.01463
589331	0.00314	-0.01102	-2.34866	2.65	0.96	-0.00190	-0.01518
717081	-0.00220	-0.02721	-1.38895	18.01	2.02	0.00499	-0.01117
806605	-0.00064	0.00465	12.12581	20.13	1.31	0.00504	-0.02947
24843	0.00126	0.01554	0.27408	6.31	1.78	0.04233	0.03925
33047	-0.00463	0.03901	-2.30515	26.22	1.64	-0.02327	0.01210
211183	0.00272	0.01400	0.33348	4.49	1.96	0.02290	0.01558
690768	0.00015	0.00831	-2.24751	1.12	2.52	-0.00043	0.00875
370514	-0.00502	0.03282	-0.67941	10.46	1.02	-0.05349	-0.04482
451542	0.00370	0.00354	16.94620	20.50	2.07	0.02613	-0.00582
524858	-0.00032	-0.00328	5.27350	2.18	1.77	-0.01457	-0.02889
542290	0.00013	0.00766	0.29425	3.34	2.01	-0.01182	-0.02029
87509	0.00102	-0.00145	-5.69153	0.34	2.48	0.06024	0.04219
760779	-0.00138	-0.01334	-0.03320	1.20	1.46	0.06478	0.06041
912656	-0.00059	-0.02790	-0.94361	2.86	1.96	0.06882	0.05077
32393	-0.00770	-0.03654	1.62144	24.96	1.84	0.02037	0.03477
489314	-0.00483	-0.09299	0.17953	32.53	1.79	0.00988	-0.00295
717265	-0.00214	-0.07422	-0.10646	21.60	1.94	0.00011	-0.01326
171196	0.00220	0.12957	-1.21326	13.77	1.48	-0.11573	-0.06911
345370	-0.00475	0.05039	-4.92821	47.97	2.03	-0.06622	-0.00565
370442	0.01221	0.09954	-1.70357	13.37	2.28	-0.11630	-0.06958

	NAIVE	MEAN	TIME	AUTO	MODEL
MAD	0.03959	0.04471	0.04329	0.03921	0.03393
MSE	0.00415	0.00400	0.00403	0.00389	0.00325

Table 7.6.

SUMMARY

	CONST.	LAMDA	DELTA	RSQ	DURB	AUTO	MODEL
276461	0.00379	0.00408	5.50695	5.93	2.45	0.09290	0.08507
725701	-0.00068	-0.01290	-2.76218	3.56	1.99	0.22546	0.22816
24703	0.00096	0.01126	-0.74411	19.11	1.79	-0.00097	-0.00160
532202	-0.00117	-0.00442	-4.98957	15.53	1.65	0.00382	-0.00251
718167	0.00412	0.00158	1.01385	1.10	1.09	-0.00605	-0.00738
761753	-0.00157	-0.00508	-3.35933	8.55	1.75	0.00320	0.00149
206813	0.00351	-0.03284	-0.69490	15.33	1.35	0.03753	0.02064
235773	-0.00245	-0.01777	1.13405	10.70	1.18	-0.01988	-0.01428
2824	-0.00241	-0.01626	0.27147	6.65	2.66	0.01283	0.01534
589331	0.00379	-0.00985	-0.77163	1.34	0.81	-0.00190	-0.00866
717081	-0.00235	-0.01906	-1.21241	20.21	1.86	0.00499	-0.00763
806605	-0.00107	-0.00843	-1.77941	1.17	0.61	0.00504	-0.01517
24843	0.00004	0.00733	-0.51779	1.67	1.70	0.04233	0.04158
33047	-0.00429	0.00764	-9.25619	52.22	0.97	-0.02327	0.01482
211183	0.00123	0.00173	-3.18258	0.31	1.73	0.02290	0.01953
690768	0.00059	0.00190	-4.14141	0.45	2.55	-0.00043	0.00621
370514	-0.00603	0.01528	-1.66447	7.01	0.88	-0.05349	-0.04204
451542	0.00119	0.01178	2.01412	15.95	1.80	0.02613	0.00267
524858	-0.00225	-0.00136	29.48175	18.11	1.43	-0.01457	-0.01501
542290	-0.00101	0.00268	-3.85451	3.08	1.67	-0.01182	-0.01501
87509	-0.00067	-0.00293	3.23577	2.41	2.32	0.06024	0.04963
760779	-0.00204	-0.01343	0.62492	6.48	1.49	0.06478	0.06569
912656	-0.00222	-0.02132	-0.32060	8.85	1.90	0.06882	0.05841
32393	-0.00422	-0.03526	1.17337	37.72	2.12	0.02037	0.03783
489314	-0.00108	-0.07715	-0.13890	42.16	2.17	0.00988	-0.00623
717265	-0.00046	-0.05961	-0.25706	34.24	2.08	0.00011	-0.01200
171196	0.00389	0.07771	-1.62989	15.42	1.51	-0.11573	-0.07029
345370	0.00090	0.02746	-7.13756	56.82	1.98	-0.06622	-0.00014
370442	0.01175	0.05438	-2.73475	21.00	2.25	-0.11630	-0.06402

	NAIVE	MEAN	TIME	AUTO	MODEL
MAD	0.03959	0.04471	0.04329	0.03921	0.03204
MSE	0.00415	0.00400	0.00403	0.00389	0.00297

Table 7.7.

SUMMARY

	CONST.	LAMDA	DELTA	RSQ	DURE	AUTO	MODEL
635655	0.01212	-0.01748	-0.62163	0.47	1.56	0.07360	0.06742
191216	-0.03137	0.04851	-0.87577	13.37	1.52	-0.03813	-0.04160
73239	-0.18217	0.15543	-1.13405	25.78	1.87	-C.18080	-0.18130
299209	-0.08856	-0.52114	0.18069	37.65	1.70	-0.33288	-0.32020
252669	0.05151	0.00436	11.24711	7.20	0.77	0.00968	0.00294
398784	0.13171	-0.10322	-1.36639	23.34	1.79	-0.43155	-0.42698
554790	-0.20978	0.05124	-3.91115	25.49	2.05	-0.00974	0.00297
457641	-0.20300	0.08815	-2.30551	14.47	2.08	0.01029	0.01785
806605	-0.11148	-0.03281	3.79414	22.64	0.93	0.00504	0.00505
54303	0.05942	0.00324	24.52826	8.85	1.79	-0.07965	-0.06624
302808	-0.27289	0.19510	-1.50858	18.99	1.46	-0.06442	-0.05369
626717	0.09242	-0.09176	-0.88183	1.67	1.23	0.03415	-0.00812
747419	0.10987	-0.15913	-0.66875	13.65	1.26	C.01209	0.00398
693506	-0.12548	0.04334	-2.93011	9.87	2.32	0.01268	-0.00318
23904	-0.09572	-0.15308	0.60508	43.47	2.88	0.00564	0.01966
489314	0.27326	-0.29681	-0.91310	10.22	2.16	0.00989	-0.01127
156825	-0.02957	-0.13444	0.22821	8.03	2.01	-0.01199	0.00534
19411	-0.27746	0.13649	-2.04824	22.08	2.01	0.01593	0.01266
307261	-0.36159	0.19440	-1.78871	15.44	2.15	0.02440	0.00835
181396	-0.06907	-0.13188	0.58421	9.85	2.44	-0.01976	-0.01864
285551	-0.46575	0.53546	-0.78325	26.50	1.81	0.18854	0.20504
984121	-0.15610	-0.03952	4.58344	17.28	1.72	-0.01721	-0.00929
631226	0.03785	-0.06228	-0.59526	6.74	1.17	-0.01525	-0.01745
746384	-0.10992	0.07503	-1.65479	12.21	1.69	-0.00865	-0.00551
884102	-0.22321	0.13394	-1.68663	16.46	2.31	0.04116	0.03802
351604	-0.05270	0.20797	-0.23483	16.16	1.67	0.00409	0.00460
268457	-0.40131	0.10258	-4.08537	31.58	2.32	-0.002C1	0.01336
361428	-0.16704	0.08210	-1.99011	19.38	2.20	0.01784	0.01013
30177	0.01312	-0.02587	-0.44530	8.86	1.24	0.00867	0.00177

	NAIVE	MEAN	TIME	AUTO	MODEL
MAD	0.05784	0.06921	0.07781	0.05813	0.05457
MSE	0.01547	0.C1556	0.01716	0.01340	0.01300

8

Conclusions

This brief, concluding chapter draws out a comparison between the model proposed here and those extant in the accounting literature. A final section draws a *finis* to this study and suggests a few areas of potential research.

A Comparison

It is of some interest to note that the proposed model is not at all unlike the models proposed to date. In general these have been of the form:

$$r_t \;=\; \theta r_{t-1} + u_t \tag{8.1}$$

where θ is close to, if not equal to one, i.e.,

$$r_t \;=\; r_{t-1} + u_t \tag{8.2}$$

In words, we encounter martingale or random walk type behavior. The proposed model, by contrast, is

$$r_t \;=\; (1-\lambda\delta)r_{t-1} + \lambda\delta_t^e - \lambda(1-\delta)\varrho_{t-1}^e + u_t \tag{8.3}$$

Assume now that ϱ_t^e is a function of past accounting rates. This is a perfectly reasonable assumption, since it is generally accepted that a major input to the formation of security prices is probably accounting earnings. A variety of specifications are possible. We assume, purely for the sake of simplicity, that

$$\varrho_t^e \;=\; r_{t-1} + u_{t-1} \tag{8.4}$$

which implies that

$$\varrho_{t-1}^e \;=\; r_{t-2} + u_{t-2} \tag{8.5}$$

Assume further, as is wholly justified by the data, that since r_{t-1} and r_{t-2} are highly correlated, we can write

$$\varrho_t^e = (r_{t-1} + w_{t-2}) + u_{t-1} \tag{8.6}$$

$$= r_{t-1} + v_{t-1} \tag{8.6}$$

Then simple substitution in (8.2) yields

$$r_t = r_{t-1} + \lambda u_{t-1} + \lambda(1-\delta)v_{t-1} \tag{8.7}$$

In other words, given the nature of the data, a random-walk model when applying Box-Jenkins's techniques to our return data would not be entirely unexpected. Alternatively, given the high degree of correlation in the data and the simultaneous equation nature of the process generating earnings, i.e., security rates are based (by hypothesis) on earnings, and earnings in turn are a function (by hypothesis) of a tendency toward security rates, it becomes difficult to disentangle a random-walk model from the model proposed.

On the other hand, the random-walk type model is a purely empirical result with little theoretical justification. This study has proposed a theoretical explanation of why we might see the empirical phenomena that we do, without reliance on the arrival of a once-a-year, wholly undefined, exogenous disturbance. Furthermore, it suggests that where autoregressive coefficients are encountered, these might be a product of a drive to equilibrium and that the coefficient might be predictable in size and sign.

Turning the discussion on its head, we can write r_t completely in terms of equilibrium rates. This is most easily done with the lag operator L. First, rewriting (8.3) we have

$$r_t = \theta_1 r_{t-1} + \theta_2 \varrho_t^e + \theta_3 \varrho_{t-1}^e$$

or

$$(1 - \theta_1 L) r_t = \theta_2 \varrho_t^e + \theta_3 \varrho_{t-1}^e$$

or

$$r_t = \frac{\theta_2}{1 - \theta_1 L} \varrho_t^e + \frac{\theta_3}{1 - \theta_1 L} \varrho_{t-1}^e$$

$$= \theta_2 (1 + \theta_1 L + \theta_1^2 L^2 + \ldots) \varrho_t^e + \theta_3 (1 + \theta_1 L + \theta_1^2 L^2 + \ldots) \varrho_{t-1}^e$$

$$= \alpha_t \varrho_t^e + \alpha_{t-1}^e \varrho_{t-1}^e + \ldots \tag{8.8}$$

In words, the observed rate might be a weighted sum of past *ex ante* equilibrium rates. This makes perfectly good sense since rates are, as we know, a mirror image of prices. We also know that the books of a firm reflect transactions over the life of that firm at the prices ruling on each transaction date. Moreover, by hypothesis there is a tendency for the firm to move to the ruling equilibrium rate, like the model I have proposed. Quite naturally, then, we should expect to arrive ultimately at a relationship of this sort.

This may be combined with Beaver's (1972) insights into the process generating earnings. Recall that he suggested that the present rate was an average of past disturbances. The suggestion here is that it is an average of past *ex ante* equilibrium rates. Due to the nature of the accounting process—Beaver says its historical cost nature while I say, more generally, its noninstantaneous response at action dates—we inevitably carry the effect of a decision in one period over into future periods. The result is a weighted average model with all the appearance of deliberate smoothing, which, of course, it is not. If Beaver is correct and the equilibrium rates follow a mean-reverting process then with

$$\varrho_t^e = \mu + u_t$$

we have

$$r_t = (\alpha_t + \alpha_{t-1} + \ldots)\mu + (\alpha_t u_t + \alpha_{t-1} u_{t-1} + \ldots) \tag{8.9}$$

Since the first term on the right is a constant and the α's decline over time the two models are quite likely to be observationally equivalent given the crudeness of our data.

In other words, the proposed model could provide a theoretical basis for the models that have been generated empirically in the literature to date. Unfortunately, the empirical results suggest strongly that the model is as yet incomplete or, alternatively, that the operationalizations are inadequate. Moreover, the collinearity between the null and alternative hypotheses has still to be resolved. Therefore, one cannot claim definitively at this point that the model provides the missing theoretical clue. Future work may resolve these issues and lead to clearer answers.

Conclusions

The analysis began with a discussion of why the prediction of corporate earnings is important. The zero-profit conditions were discussed and the work of J. S. Bain on barriers to entry introduced. A model was hypothesized to capture the adjustment process discussed by Bain and an alternative hypothesis based on accounting factors was offered. The model was tested against data.

The model did not behave as well as expected. Using security specific rates, the signs of the adjustment parameters were of the correct sign with one exception. However, the explanatory power was generally low, as was the predictive power of the model. It does appear, though, that the rates of reversion are indeed negatively correlated with book lives, as predicted.

The high degree of collinearity between the null and alternative hypothesis, together with the weakness of the results, prevents any definite conclusion from being drawn. Clearly, if the alternative hypothesis could be demonstrated, the policy implications would be enormous, because barrier-to-entry arguments have long been used as policy instruments. However, only further work in this area will prove the superiority of one or the other hypothesis.

Several lines need further investigation. First, a better, more theoretically specified definition of the expected market return must be derived. This might include building industry-specific rates from the CRSP tape. Second, it is imperative that the factors that are biasing the delta parameter be controlled. Third, the operationalization of asset life might be improved and the growth factor accounted for. This is becoming more possible now that replacement cost data are becoming available, since companies are obliged to show depreciation on a straight-line basis. This will remove the bias inherent when one does not know the depreciation basis used. Finally, it will be imperative to collect extra data that will enable the present collinearity between the null and the alternative hypotheses to be broken.

Bibliography

Adelman, I.G., "A Stochastic Analysis of the Size Distribution of Firms," *Journal of the American Statistical Association,* 53:893-904, 1958.

AICPA Objectives Committee, *Objectives of Financial Statements,* New York, American Institute of Certified Public Accounts, 1973.

Aitchison, J., and J.A.C. Brown, *The Log-Normal Distribution,* Cambridge University Press, 1957.

Albrecht, W.S., L.L. Lookabill, and J.S. McKeown, "The Time Series Properties of Annual Earnings," Working Paper, University of Illinois, 1975.

Allen, R.G.D., *Macro-Economic Theory: A Mathematical Treatment,* New York, St. Martin's Press, 1968.

Anderson, T.W., *The Statistical Analysis of Time Series,* New York, John Wiley, 1971.

Arrow, K.J., *Essays in the Theory of Risk-Bearing,* Chicago, Markham, 1971.

_____., "The Role of Securities in the Optimal Allocation of Risk-Bearing," *Review of Economic Studies,* 31:91-96, 1964.

_____., *Social Choice and Individual Values,* Cowles Foundation Monograph 12, New York, John Wiley, 1963.

_____., "Toward a Theory of Price Adjustment," in *The Allocation of Economic Resources,* editor: M. Abramovitz, Stanford University Press, 1959.

_____., and F.H. Hahn, *General Competitive Analysis,* San Francisco, Holden Day, 1971.

Bain, J.S., *Barriers to New Competition,* Harvard University Press, 1956.

Ball, R., and P. Brown, "An Empirical Evaluation of Accounting Income Numbers," *Journal of Accounting Research,* 6:159-78, 1968.

_____., and R. Watts, "Some Time Series Properties of Accounting Income," *Journal of Finance,* 27:663-82, 1972.

Beaver, W.H., "Alternative Accounting Measures as Predictors of Failure," *Accounting Review,* 45:113-22, 1968.

_____., "The Behavior of Security Prices and its Implications for Accounting Research (Methods)," *Accounting Review Supplement,* 47:407-37, 1972.

_____., "The Evolution of Security Price Research in Accounting," Stanford University Working Paper, 1974.

_____., "Financial Ratios as Predictions of Failure," *Empirical Research in Accounting: Selected Studies,* 1966, Supplement to *Journal of Accounting Research,* 4:71-111, 1966.

_____., "Financial Statements: Issues of Preparation and Interpretation," Stanford University Working Paper, 1975.

_____., "Implications of Security Price Research for Accounting: A Reply to Bierman," *Accounting Review,* 49:563-71, 1974.

_____., "The Information Content of Annual Earnings Announcements," *Journal of Accounting Research Supplement,* 6:67-92, 1968.

_____., "The Information Content of the Magnitude of Unexpected Earnings," Stanford University Working Paper, 1974.

_____., "Market Prices, Financial Ratios and the Prediction of Failure," *Journal of Accounting Research,* 6:179-92, 1968.

————., "The Time Series Behavior of Earnings," *Journal of Accounting Research* (Supplement), 8:62-99, 1970.

————., "What Should be the Objectives of the FASB?", *Journal of Accountancy*, 136:49-56, 1973.

————., and J. Demski, "The Nature of Financial Accounting Objectives," *Journal of Accounting Research* (Supplement), 12:170-87, 1974.

————., and R.E. Dukes, "Delta-Depreciation Methods: Some Analytical Results," *Journal of Accounting Research*, 12:205-15, 1974.

————., J.W. Kenelly, and W.M. Voss, "Predictive Ability as a Criterion for the Evaluation of Accounting Data," *The Accounting Review*, 43:675-83, 1968.

————., P. Kettler, and M. Scholes, "The Association between Market Determined and Accounting Determined Risk Measures," *The Accounting Review*, 45:654-82, 1970.

————., and J. Manegold, "The Association between Market Determined and Accounting Determined Measures of Systematic Risk: Some Further Evidence," *Journal of Finance and Quantitative Analysis*, 10:231-84, 1975.

Bedford, N.M., *Income Determination Theory: An Accounting Framework*, Reading, MA, Addison-Wesley, 1965.

Bliss, C.J., *Capital Theory and the Distribution of Income*, Amsterdam, North-Holland, 1975.

Box, G.E.P., and G.M. Jenkins, *Time Series Analysis, Forecasting and Control*, San Francisco, Holden Day, 1970.

Brealey, R.A., *An Introduction to Risk and Return from Common Stocks*, Cambridge, M.I.T. Press, 1969.

————., *Security Prices in a Competitive Market*, Cambridge, M.I.T. Press, 1971.

Champernowne, D.G., *The Distribution of Income between Persons*, Cambridge University Press, 1973.

————., "A Model of Income Distribution," *Economic Journal*, 63:318-51, 1953.

Collins, N.R., and L.E. Preston, *Concentration and Price Cost Margins in Manufacturing Industries*, Berkeley, University of California Press, 1968.

Cootner, P.M., and D. Holland, "Rate of Return and Business Risk," *Bell Journal of Economics and Management Science*, 1:211-26, 1970.

Cragg, J.G., and B.G. Malkiel, "The Consensus and Accuracy of Some Predictions of the Growth of Corporate Earnings," *Journal of Finance*, 23:67-84, 1968.

Cramer, J.S., *Empirical Econometrics*, Amsterdam, North-Holland, 1969.

Dhrymes, P.J., *Econometrics*, New York, Springer-Verlag, 1974.

Dopuch N., and R. Watts, "Using Time-Series Models to Assess the Significance of Accounting Changes," *Journal of Accounting Research*, 10:180-94, 1972.

Durbin, J., "An Alternative to the Bounds Test for Testing Serial Correlation in Least-squares Regression," *Econometrica*, 38:422-29, 1970.

Esposito, L., and F.F. Esposito, "Foreign Competition and Domestic Industry Profitability," *Review of Economics and Statistics*, 53:343-53, 1971.

Fama, E.F., and M.H. Miller, *The Theory of Finance*, New York, Holt, Rinehart and Winston, 1972.

Ferguson, C.E., *The Neoclassical Theory of Production and Distribution*, Cambridge University Press, 1969.

Financial Accounting Standards Board, *Tentative Conclusions on Objectives of Financial Statements of Business Enterprises*, 1976.

Foster, G., "Quarterly Accounting Data: Time-Series Properties and Predictive-Ability Results," *Accounting Review*, 52:1-22, 1977.

Frank, W., "A Study of the Predictive Significance of Two Income Measures," *Journal of Accounting Research*, 7:123-36, 1969.

Gale, B.T., "Market Share and Rate of Return," *Review of Economics and Statistics,* 54:412-23, 1972.

Granger, C.W.J., *Spectral Analysis of Economic Time Series,* Princeton University Press, 1964.

Griffin, P.A. "The Time Series Behavior of Quarterly Earnings: Preliminary Evidence," Unpublished paper, Stanford University, 1975.

Griliches, Z., "A Note on the Serial Correlation Bias in Estimates of Distributed Lags," *Econometrica,* 29:65-73, 1961.

Hall, M. and L.W. Weiss, "Firm Size and Profitability," *Review of Economics and Statistics,* 49:319-31, 1967.

Hamada, R.S. "The Effect of the Firm's Capital Structure on the Systematic Risk of Common Stocks," *Journal of Finance,* 27:435-52, 1972.

Hanushek, E.A., "Efficient Estimators for Regressing Regression Coefficients," *The American Statistician,* 28:66-67, 1974.

Harcourt, G.C., "The Accountant in a Golden Age," *Oxford Economic Papers,* 17:66-80, 1965.

Harrison, M.J., "The Power of the Durbin-Weston and Geary Tests: Comment and Further Evidence," *Review of Economics and Statistics,* 57:377-79, 1975.

Hayek, F.A., *Individualism and Economic Order,* Chicago, Gateway Edition, 1972.

Hicks, J.R., *Capital and Growth,* Oxford University Press, 1965.

Hirshleifer, J., *Investment, Interest and Capital,* Englewood Cliffs, N.J., Prentice-Hall, 1970.

Hurwicz, L., "Least Squares Bias in Time Series," in *Statistical Inference in Dynamic Economic Models,* T.C. Koopmans, ed., Cowles Commission Monograph No. 10, J. Wiley and Sons, New York, 1950.

Ijiri, Y., and H.A. Simon, "Business Firm Growth and Size," *American Economic Review,* 54:77-89, 1964.

Jensen, M.C., "Discussions of the Time Series Behavior of Earnings," *Journal of Accounting Research* (Supplement), 8:100-103, 1970.

Jevons, W.S., *The Theory of Political Economy (1871),* Harmondsworth, England, Penguin Books, 1970.

Jonkheere, A.R., "A Distribution-Free *K*-Sample Test Against Ordered Alternatives," *Biometrika,* 41:133-45, 1954.

Kalecki, M., "On the Gibrat Distribution," *Econometrica,* 13:161-70, 1945.

———., *Theory of Economic Dynamics,* Second edition, London, Allen and Unwin, 1965.

Kendall, M.G., *Time-Series,* London, Griffin, 1973.

Kenkel, J.L., "Some Small Sample Properties of Durbin's Tests for Serial Correlation in Regression Models Containing Lagged Dependent Variables," *Econometrica,* 42:763-69, 1974.

Keynes, J.M., *The General Theory of Employment, Interest and Money (1935),* New York, Harcourt, Brace and World, 1964.

King, B.F., "Market and Industry Factors in Stock Price Behavior," *Journal of Business,* 39:139-90, 1966.

Knight, F.H., *Risk, Uncertainty and Profit,* University of Chicago Press, 1971.

Koopmans, T.C., *Three Essays on the State of Economic Science,* New York, McGraw-Hill, 1957.

Kuhn, T.S., *The Structure of Scientific Revolutions,* University of Chicago Press, 1962.

Lev, B., "Industry Averages as Targets for Financial Ratios," *Journal of Accounting Research,* 7:290-99, 1969.

Litzenberger, R., and A. Budd, "Corporate Investment Criteria and the Value of Risk Assets," *Journal of Financial and Quantitative Analysis,* 5:395-419, 1970.

———., and O.M. Joy, "Further Evidence of the Persistence of Corporate Profitability Rates," *Western Economic Journal,* 8:209-12, 1970.

Lorek, K.S., C.L. McDonald, and D. Patz, "A Comparative Examination of Management Forecasts and Box-Jenkins Forecasts of Earnings," *Accounting Review,* 51:321-30, 1976.

Malinvaud, E., "The Estimation of Distributed Lags: A Comment," *Econometrica,* 29:430-33, 1961.

_____., *Statistical Methods of Econometrics,* Second edition, Amsterdam, North-Holland, 1970.

Malkiel, B.G., and J.G. Cragg, "Expectations and the Structure of Share Prices," *American Economic Review,* 60:601-17, 1970.

Mandelbrot, B., "The Pareto-Levey Law and the Distribution of Income," *International Economic Review,* 1:79-106, 1960.

_____., "Stable Pareto Random Functions and the Multiplicative Variation of Income," *Econometrica,* 29:517-43, 1961.

Manegold, James G., "Time-Series Models of the Components of Earnings," AISRP Working Paper #80-2, September 1979.

Mann, H.M., "Seller Concentration, Barriers to Entry, and Rates of Return in Thirty Industries, 1950-1960," *Review of Economics and Statistics,* 48:296-307, 1966.

Markowitz, H., "Portfolio Selection," *Journal of Finance,* 9:77-91, 1952.

Marshall, A., *Principles of Economics,* Eighth edition, (1920), London, Macmillian, 1974.

Means, G.C., "Simultaneous Inflation and Unemployment: A Challenge to Theory and Policy," *Challenge,* 18:6-20, 1975.

Modigliani, F., and E. Grunberg, "The Predictability of Social Events," *Journal of Political Economy,* 62:465-78, 1954.

_____., and M.H. Miller, "Corporate Income Taxes and the Cost of Capital: A Correction," *American Economic Review,* 53:433-43, 1963.

_____., and M.H. Miller, "The Cost of Capital, Corporation Finance and the Theory of Investment," *American Economic Review,* 48:261-97, 1958.

_____., and M.H. Miller, "Some Estimates of the Cost of Capital to the Electric Utility Industry, 1954-1957," *American Economic Review,* 56:333-91, 1966.

Mood, A.M., D.C. Boes, and F.A. Graybill, *Introduction to the Theory of Statistics,* Third edition, New York, McGraw-Hill, 1974.

Morgan, I.G., "Prediction of Return with the Minimum Variance Zero-Beta Portfolio," *Journal of Financial Economics,* 2:361-76, 1975.

Mossin, J., "Equilibrium in a Capital Asset Market," *Econometrica,* 34:768-83, 1966.

_____., "Optimal Multiperiod Portfolio Policies," *Journal of Business,* 41:215-29, 1968.

_____., *Theory of Financial Markets,* Englewood Cliffs, N.J., Prentice-Hall, 1973.

Muth, J.F., "Rational Expectations and the Theory of Price Movements," *Econometrica,* 29:315-35, 1961.

Nelson, C.R. *Applied Time Series Analysis,* San Francisco, Holden-Day, 1973.

O'Hagan, J., and B. McCabe, "Tests for the Security of Multicollinearity in Regression Analysis: A Comment," *Review of Economics and Statistics,* 57:368-70, 1975.

Orr, D., "The Determinants of Entry: A Study of the Canadian Manufacturing Industries," *Review of Economics and Statistics,* 56:58-66, 1974.

Parzen, E., *Stochastic Processes,* San Francisco, Holden-Day, 1962.

Quirk, J., and R. Saposnik, *Introduction to General Equilibrium Theory and Welfare Economics,* New York, McGraw-Hill, 1968.

Racette, G.A., "Earnings Retention, New Capital and the Growth of the Firm: A Comment," *Review of Economics and Statistics,* 55:127-28, 1973.

Rao, P., "Some Notes on Misspecification in Multiple Regression," *The American Statistician,* 25:37-39, 1971.

Rayner, A.C., and I.M.D. Little. *Higgledy Piggledy Growth Again,* Oxford University Press, 1966.

Reiersøl, O., "Identifiability of a Linear Relation Between Variables which are Subject to Error," *Econometrica,* 18:375-89, 1950.

Revsine, L., *Replacement Cost Accounting,* Englewood Cliffs, N.J., Prentice-Hall, 1973.

Reynolds, L.G., "Relations Between Wage Rates, Costs and Prices," *American Economic Review* (Supplement), 32:275-89, 1942.

Rhoades, S.A., "The Effect of Diversification on Industry Profit Performance in 241 Manufacturing Industries: 1963," *Review of Economics and Statistics,* 55:146-55, 1973.

Romeo, A.A., "Interindustry and Interfirm Differences in the Rate of Diffusion of an Innovation," *Review of Economics and Statistics,* 57:311-19, 1975.

Rosenberg, B., and W. McKibben, "The Prediction of Systematic and Specific Risk in Common Stocks," *Journal of Financial and Quantitative Analysis,* 8:317-33, 1973.

Rosenblatt, M., *Random Processes,* Oxford University Press, 1962.

Samuelson, P.A., *Foundations of Economic Analysis (1943),* New York, Atheneum College Edition, 1972.

Sandilands, Report, *Inflation Accounting: Report of the Inflation Accounting Committee,* London, HMSO, 1975.

Sarnat, M., and H. Levy, "The Relationship of Rules of Thumb to the Internal Rate of Return: A Restatement and Generalization," *Journal of Finance,* 24:479-90, 1969.

Savage, L.J., *The Foundations of Statistics,* Second revised edition, New York, Dover, 1972.

Schmidt, P., "A Note on Theil's Minimum Standard Error Criterion when the Disturbances are Autocorrelated," *Review of Economics and Statistics,* 56:122-23, 1974.

————., and D.R. Guilkey, "Some Further Evidence on the Power of the Durbin-Watson and Geary Tests," *Review of Economics and Statistics,* 57:379-82, 1975.

Schumpeter, J.A., *The Theory of Economic Development (1911),* Oxford University Press, 1961.

Scitovszky, T., de, "A Note on Welfare Propositions in Economics," *Review of Economic Studies,* 9:77-88, 1941-42.

Shackle, G.L.S., *Expectation, Enterprise and Profit,* Chicago, Aldine, 1970.

Sharpe, W.F., "Capital Asset Prices: A Theory of Market Equilibrium under Conditions of Risk," *Journal of Finance,* 19:425-42, 1964.

————., *Portfolio Theory and Capital Markets,* New York, McGraw-Hill, 1970.

Sherman, R., and R. Tollison, "Advertising and Profitability," *Review of Economics and Statistics,* 53:397-407, 1971.

Simmons, J.K., and J. Gray, "An Investigation of the Effect of Differing Accounting Frameworks on the Prediction of Income," *The Accounting Review,* 44:757-76, 1969.

Simon, H., and C.R. Bonini, "The Size Distribution of Business Firms," *American Economic Review,* 48:607-17, 1958.

Singh, A., and G. Whittington, *Growth, Profitability and Valuation,* Cambridge University Press, 1968.

Slutzky, E., "The Summation of Random Causes as the Source of Cyclic Processes," *Econometrica,* 5:105-46, 1937.

Solomon, E., "Arithmetic of Capital Budgeting Decisions," *Journal of Business,* 29:124-29, 1956.

Solow, R.M., "A Contribution to the Theory of Econometric Growth," *Quarterly Journal of Economics,* 70:65-94, 1956.

Sorter, G.H. "An 'Events' Approach to Basic Accounting Theory," *Accounting Review,* 44:12-19, 1969.

Sraffa, P., *Production of Commodities by Means of Commodities: Prelude to a Critique of Economic Theory,* Cambridge University Press, 1960.

Stauffer, T.A., "The Measurement of Corporate Rates of Return: A Generalized Foundation," *Bell Journal of Economics and Management Science,* 2:434-69, 1971.

Steindl, J., *Random Processes and the Growth of Firms,* New York, Hafner, 1965.

Stigler, G.J., *Capital and Rates of Return in Manufacturing Industries,* Princeton University Press, 1963.

———., *The Theory of Price,* Third edition, New York, Macmillan, 1966.

Swalm, R.O., "On Calculating the Rate of Return on Investment," *The Journal of Industrial Engineering,* 9:99-103, 1958.

Swan, T.W., "Economic Growth and Capital Accumulation," *Economic Research,* 32:334-61, 1956.

Theil, H., *Economic Forecasts and Policy,* Amsterdam, North-Holland, 1961.

———., *Principles of Econometrics,* New York, John Wiley, 1971.

Tobin, J., and W.C. Brainard, "Asset Markets and the Cost of Capital," Yale University Working Paper, 1975.

Van Breda, M.F., and J.L. Livingstone, "The Relationship Between Accounting and the Internal Rate of Return Measures: A Reply," *Journal of Accounting Research,* 14:187-88, 1976.

Watts, R.L. "The Time Series Behavior of Accounting Earnings," Appendix A to "The Information Content of Dividends," Ph.D. dissertation, The University of Chicago, 1971.

———., "The Time Series Behavior of Quarterly Earnings," University of Newcastle Working Paper, 1975.

Weiss, L.M., "Factors in Changing Concentration," *Review of Economics and Statistics,* 55: 70-77, 1973.

———., "Quantitative Studies of Industrial Organizations," in M. Intriligator, *Frontiers of Quantitative Economics,* Amsterdam, North-Holland, 1971.

Weston, J.F., "The Profit Concept and Theory: A Restatement," *Journal of Political Economy,* 62:152-70, 1954.

Whittington, G., "The Profitability of Retained Earnings," *Review of Economics and Statistics,* 54:152-60, 1972.

Wichers, R.C., "The Determination of Multicollinearity: A Comment," *Review of Economics and Statistics,* 57:366-68, 1975.

Wicksell, K., *Value, Capital and Rent (1895),* New York, Augustus Kelley, 1970

———., *Lectures on Political Economy (1911),* New York, Augustus Kelley, 1967.

Wold, H.O.A., and P. Whittle, "A Model Explaining the Pareto Distribution of Wealth," *Econometrica,* 25:291-595, 1957.

Zellner, A., and H. Thornber, "Computational Accuracy and Estimation of Simultaneous Equation Econometric Models," *Econometrica,* 34:427-29, 1966.

Index